Science Projects About

Temperature and Heat

Robert Gardner
and
Eric Kemer

● Science Projects ●

ENSLOW PUBLISHERS, INC.

44 Fadem Road   P.O. Box 38
Box 699   Aldershot
Springfield, N.J. 07081   Hants GU12 6BP
U.S.A.   U.K.

Library of Congress Cataloging-in-Publication Data

Gardner, Robert, 1929–
    Science projects about temperature and heat / by Robert Gardner
and Eric Kemer.
        p. cm. — (Science projects)
    Includes bibliographical references and index.
    ISBN 0-89490-534-1
    1. Temperature—Experiments—Juvenile literature. 2. Heat—
Experiments—Juvenile literature. 3. Science projects—Juvenile
literature. 4. Science—Exhibitions—Juvenile literature.
    [1. Temperature—Experiments. 2. Heat—Experiments.
3. Experiments. 4. Science projects. 5. Science—Exhibitions.]
I. Kemer, Eric. II. Title. III. Series: Gardner, Robert, 1929–
Science projects.
    QC271.4.G37   1994
    536'.078—dc20   93-48800
                                                            CIP
                                                            AC
Printed in the United States of America

10 9 8 7 6 5 4 3

Illustration Credits: Stephen F. Delisle

Cover Illustration: © Stuart Simons, 1994

Contents

*appropriate for science fair project ideas

appropriate for science fair project ideas

Introduction

The science projects and experiments in this book have to do with temperature and heat. You will find as much emphasis on the processes of science as you will on temperature and heat. That is because we want you to understand how science proceeds—how theories are made and their consequences tested—as much as we want you to understand temperature and heat.

As you do these projects, you will find it useful to record your ideas, notes, data, and anything you can conclude from your experiments in a notebook. In that way, you can keep track of the information you gather and the conclusions you reach. It will allow you to refer back to other experiments you have done that may be useful to you in projects you will do later.

Science Fairs

Some of the projects in this book might be appropriate for a science fair. Those projects are indicated with an asterisk (*). However, judges at such fairs do not reward projects or experiments that are simply copied from a book. For example, a model of a thermometer would probably not impress judges unless it was done in a novel or creative way. A model explaining the nature of heat, similar to the one found in this book, would receive more consideration than a rigid papier-mâché model.

Science fair judges tend to reward creative thought and imagination. However, it is difficult to be creative or imaginative unless you are really interested in your project, so choose something that appeals to you. Consider, too, your own ability and the cost of materials needed for the project.

If you decide to use a project found in this book for a science fair, you will need to find ways to modify or extend the project. This should not be difficult because you will probably find that as you do these projects new ideas for experiments will come to mind. These new experiments could make excellent science fair projects, particularly because they spring from your own mind and are interesting to you.

If you decide to enter a science fair and have never entered one, you should read some of the books listed in the bibliography on page 124. The references that deal specifically with science fairs will provide plenty of helpful hints and lots of useful information that will enable you to avoid the pitfalls that sometimes plague first-time entrants. You will learn how to prepare appealing reports that include charts and graphs, how to set up and display your work, how to present your project, and how to relate to judges and visitors.

Safety First

Most of the projects in this book are safe. However, the following safety rules are well worth reading and remembering before you start any project.

1. Do all experiments or projects, whether from this book or of your own design, under the supervision of a science teacher or other knowledgeable adult.

2. Read all instructions carefully before proceeding with a project. If you have questions, check with your supervisor before going any further.

3. Maintain a serious attitude while conducting experiments. Fooling around can be dangerous to you and to others.

4. Wear approved safety goggles when you are doing anything that might cause injury to your eyes.

5. Do not eat or drink while experimenting.

6. Have a first aid kit nearby while you are experimenting.

7. Do not put your fingers or any object in electrical outlets.

8. Never experiment with household electricity except under the supervision of a knowledgeable adult.

9. Do not touch a lit bulb. Light bulbs produce light and they also produce heat.

10. Keep flammable materials such as alcohol away from flames and other sources of heat.

11. If you are using matches or flames, wear safety goggles and have a fire extinguisher and a fire blanket nearby and know how to use them.

12. Do not touch glassware that has been heated. Use insulated gloves or metal tongs when appropriate. If you should get burned, rinse the burn with cold water and apply ice.

13. If a thermometer breaks, inform your adult supervisor. Do not touch either the mercury or the broken glass with your bare hands.

1

Temperature

The temperature of objects, that is, their hotness or coldness, is an important factor. If the air is a bit too warm or too cool, people will change their clothes or adjust their house thermostats. If food is too hot or too cold, eating becomes very unpleasant. People react to changes in temperature for good reasons. Slight changes in the temperature of the human body can be signs of illness and can even cause death. The same is true for many other living things.

Beyond comfort and health, our modern way of life depends on our ability to control temperature. The manufacture of almost every synthetic material requires the careful control of temperature. Our ability to refrigerate food allows it to be preserved and shipped to places far from the farms that grow it.

Since temperature plays such an important role in our lives, we should try to understand it. In this chapter you will carry out a number of investigations that will help you gain a better understanding of temperature.

Temperature by Touch

Our first experiences with temperature are based on our sense of touch. By touching objects we learn to tell hot from cold and to become familiar with the many levels in between. Sometimes our lessons are painful—we burn a finger on a hot stove or shiver after diving into a cold lake. During investigation 1–1 you will learn about temperature by touch.

1.1 Experiencing Temperature by Touch

You probably think that your skin and fingers can tell hot from cold. However, you may change your mind after you do the following experiment.

(1) Fill one of the bowls or pans two-thirds full with *cool* water from the tap and set it on a table. Fill another bowl one-third with *cold* tap water. Then add ice cubes until the second bowl is also two-thirds full.

Things you'll need:

- three large bowls or pans
- tap water
- tray of ice cubes
- flat metal pan
- a block of wood
- piece of cloth (wool or cotton)

(2) Dry your hands thoroughly. Then put your *right* hand into the bowl containing the cool tap water.

Describe what you feel. Does the feeling change if you keep your hand very still for a minute or two? How does the feeling change when you swirl your hand in the bowl? Can you describe the temperature you feel in both cases?

(3) Now place your *right* hand into the ice water. How does this feeling compare with the one you experienced with the cool tap water? Can you describe how much colder the ice water is than the cool tap water? What does "ice-cold" feel like?

(4) Fill the third bowl two-thirds full with hot water from the tap. Place your left hand into the hot water. **Be sure not to burn yourself. If the water is too hot, wait for it to cool down a bit.** Describe what you feel.

How does this feeling compare with the feelings of cool water and ice cold water? What does hot feel like? Does the feeling change as time passes? How would you describe to someone the difference between hot and cold?

(5) Place the three bowls side by side with the hot water on your right, the ice water on your left, and the cool water in the middle (See

Figure 1-1). If the hot water has cooled, refill the bowl again with hot water.

(6) Dry your hands thoroughly. Then place your *right* hand in the hot water and your *left* hand in the ice water. Hold them completely under the water for three minutes.

(7) Remove your hands from the bowls and put both of them into the bowl of cool water. How does the water feel to your *right* hand? How does it feel to your *left* hand? Is it possible for the cool tap water to have two different temperatures at the same time?

(8) After your hands are dry, place the metal pan, block of wood, and piece of cloth side by side on a dry table top. Since all these objects have been sitting in the same room for a long time, we should expect them to have the same temperature.

Press the palm of your right hand against each object in turn. Which object feels coldest? Which object feels warmest? How can you explain these results?

hot water   cool water   ice water

Figure 1-1) Measuring temperature by touch.

A Simple Way to Measure Temperature

Your first investigation of temperature may have been very confusing. Even though you can tell hot from cold, it is difficult to describe the difference in words. You may also have found it difficult to understand how one hand can feel cold and the other warm when both are in the same water. This experience should not discourage you. Answering difficult questions and overcoming confusion is what science is all about.

Since it is difficult to describe temperature from your sense of touch, you must find a better way. You must measure temperature by its effect on something other than your body and how it feels to you. Descriptions based on measurable effects that are independent of personal feelings are called *objective*. Descriptions based on personal feelings, such as our sense of touch or taste, are called *subjective*. Although both are real, objective descriptions have greater scientific value because *they are the same for everyone*.

When you measure something, you compare it with a standard amount, or *unit*, of something else. For example, when you measure the length of a table top, you compare it with a ruler, which is marked off in standard units of length, such as centimeters or inches. Length is then measured by counting the number of these standard units. We measure the time it takes for something to happen by comparing it to the standard units of time (seconds, minutes, or hours) that a clock "ticks off."

Since you already know how to measure length, let us try to measure temperature changes by measuring changes in the length of something.

1.2 Temperature Effects on the Length of Wires*

To find out how the lengths of metal wires change when their temperatures increase, carry out the following experiment (see Figure 1-2). **Ask an adult to help you because you will be using matches and candles.**

(1) Hammer one of the nails into each of the two wooden blocks. Set up the tables about 8 ft (2.5 m) apart as shown in Figure 1-2. Use the C-clamps to attach the blocks to the tables.

(2) Cut a 10 ft (3 m) length of the steel wire. Thread one end of the wire through the washer and twist it back around itself several times. Then thread the rubber band through the washer and loop its two ends over the nail in the first block.

Things you'll need:

- two large nails
- two blocks of wood—2 x 4 x 12 in (5 x 10 x 30 cm)
- two C-clamps
- two tables
- about 10 ft (3 m) of 18-gauge steel and aluminum wire (copper or brass may be substituted for one of these if necessary)
- one small steel washer
- one heavy rubber band
- pencil
- four small candles

(3) Twist the other end of the wire around the nail in the second block. Then carefully push the tables apart until the wire is straight and the rubber band is stretched almost to its limit.

(4) Bend the tip of the excess wire near the washer so that it forms a pointer directed straight down toward the surface of the block. Use the pencil to mark the block directly beneath the end of the wire.

(5) Have two friends, **under the supervision of an adult**, help you slowly move the flames of four lighted candles back and forth along the length of the wire. Carefully observe the pointer's position. Did the wire get longer or shorter when its temperature increased? How much did its length change?

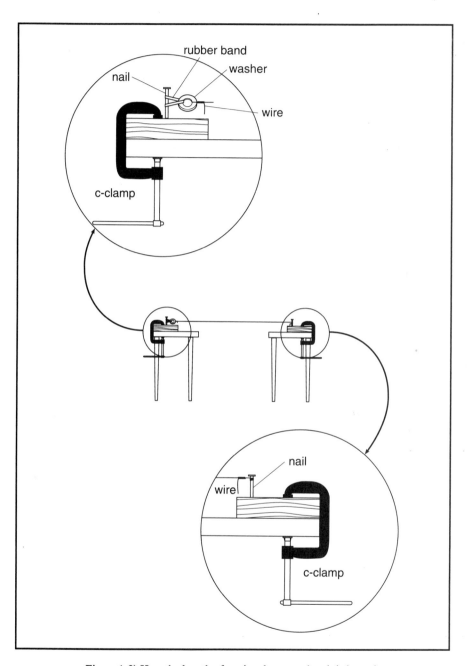

Figure 1-2) How the length of a wire changes when it is heated.

(6) Repeat the experiment, **under adult supervision,** with aluminum wire. Be sure to use the same length of wire and the same number of candles.

Does the length of the aluminum wire change when it is heated? How did the change in length of the aluminum wire compare with the steel wire? By how much do you think the wires will change if they are only half as long? Test your prediction, **under adult supervision,** by repeating the experiment with wires half as long. Were you right?

What will happen if two different metals are bonded together and heated?

Exploring on Your Own

- Fill two 2-liter soda bottles with water, sand, or gravel. Place the bottles on a long table, a kitchen counter, or the floor. Connect a long piece of thin copper, brass, aluminum, or iron wire to each bottle by tying the ends of the wire around their necks. Move the bottles apart until the wire is taut. Use a short piece of wire to hang a weight, such as a fishing sinker, from the center of the wire. With a ruler, measure the height of the center of the wire above the table, counter, or floor. **With an adult present,** light a candle and use it to heat the wire by moving the flame back and forth along the wire. As the wire is heated, continue to measure its height. Why does the height of the center of the wire decrease as the temperature of the wire increases? What do you predict will happen to the height of the wire's center as the wire cools back to room temperature?

1.3 The Effect of Temperature on Liquid Volume*

To find out how liquids change when their temperatures rise or fall, carry out the following steps.

(1) Fill the test tube to the brim with the colored water.

(2) Coat the one end of the drinking straw with some of the petroleum jelly. Push this end of the straw through the hole in the rubber stopper. If you do not have a rubber stopper use modeling clay or plasticine to make a plug.

(3) Insert the rubber stopper or clay plug into the mouth of the test tube and push it firmly into place. The water level should rise about halfway up the drinking straw (See Figure 1-3).

(4) Use the scissors to cut a strip of cardboard the length of the straw. Tape the cardboard strip to the straw as shown in Figure 1-3. Let the test tube stand for ten minutes. Then mark the water level on the cardboard with the pencil or marking pen.

Things you'll need:

- one large test tube and test tube holder
- single-hole rubber stopper to fit test tube, modeling clay, or plasticine
- a cup of water with a few drops of food coloring added
- transparent plastic drinking straw that fits snugly in the stopper hole
- petroleum jelly
- scissors
- strip of thin cardboard
- tape
- two large plastic containers (8-16 oz)
- pencil or marking pen
- hot and cold tap water
- ruler
- rubbing alcohol

(5) Place the test tube in one of the large plastic containers filled with hot tap water. Observe the water level in the straw. Mark its final level and measure the change in height with the ruler.

(6) Remove the test tube from the hot water and place it in another

container filled with cold water. Observe and mark the final water level in the straw.

What happens to the *volume*, the amount of space filled by the water, when the temperature increases? What happens to the volume of the water when the temperature decreases?

How do you think the water levels in the straw would change if the straw were thinner? Do you think the change in water level would be different if the test tube were twice as wide? Half as wide?

(7) Repeat the above experiment using the rubbing alcohol in the test tube. Be sure to refill the plastic container with "fresh" hot water. Does alcohol behave like water when its temperature increases and decreases? Are there any differences in the behavior of these two liquids when they are heated or cooled?

You have seen how changes in temperature affect the volume of solids and liquids. Perhaps you can predict how changes in temperature will affect the volume of a gas such as air. In the next project you will have an opportunity to test your prediction.

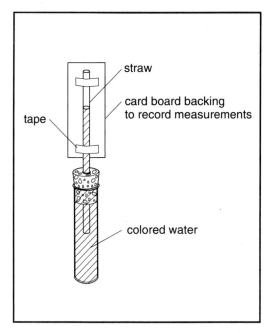

Figure 1-3) How heating and cooling affect the volume of a liquid.

1.4 How Temperature Affects the Volume of Air*

The effect of temperature changes on the volume of a gas such as air can be seen by carrying out the following experiment.

(1) Coat one end of the drinking straw with petroleum jelly. Push this end of the straw through the hole in the rubber stopper. If you do not have a rubber stopper, make a plug out of modeling clay or plasticine.

(2) Holding the straw sideways, use the eye dropper to inject a drop or two of the colored water into one end. The drops should form a water "plug" that fills a small section of the straw, as shown in Figure 1-4a.

Things you'll need:

- one large test tube
- single-hole rubber stopper to fit test tube, modeling clay, or plasticine
- transparent plastic drinking straw that fits snugly in the stopper hole
- petroleum jelly
- two large plastic containers (8-16 oz)
- pencil or marking pen
- hot and cold tap water
- eye dropper
- cup of water with a few drops of food coloring added

(3) Tilt the straw slightly more upright to allow the water plug to slide down to a position just above the stopper. Then place one finger firmly over the top of the straw and hold it in an upright position. Your finger will keep the water plug from falling farther downward in the straw as shown in Figure 1-4b.

(4) With your finger still sealing the top of the straw, insert the rubber stopper or clay plug into the mouth of the empty test tube. When you release your finger, the water plug should rise to about the center of the straw and remain there, as shown in Figure 1-4c.

(5) Use the pencil or pen to mark the level of the bottom of the water plug on the straw. If the water plug slides down, it means there

is an air leak in the straw around the rubber stopper that must be sealed with petroleum jelly.

(6) Place the test tube in a container of hot water. Watch the level of the water plug as the hot water warms the air in the test tube. What happens to the volume of the air as its temperature rises?

How does the change in the volume of the air compare with the changes in volume you found for water and alcohol? How does the speed at which the volume of a gas changes compare with the speed at which the volume of a liquid changes?

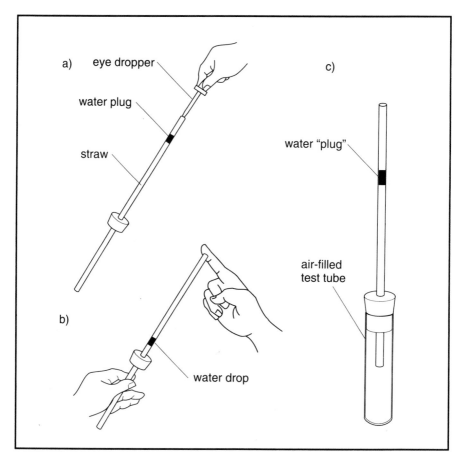

Figure 1-4) Making an air thermometer.

(7) Repeat the experiment, but this time place the test tube in a cup of very cold water. What happens to the volume of the air when its temperature decreases?

Exploring on Your Own

- If the test tube in investigation 1.4 were smaller, do you think the level of the water plug would change more or less? You can make the volume of air smaller by partially filling the test tube with water. Repeat the experiment with the test tube almost filled with water. What do you observe about the change in volume this time?

- Pull the neck of an empty balloon over the mouth of a large glass or rigid plastic bottle. Predict what will happen to the balloon if you place the bottle in a pan of hot water. Test your prediction. Were you right?

- What do you think will happen to the balloon if you place the bottle in a refrigerator? Again, test your prediction by experimenting. Were you right this time?

Thermal Expansion and Other Temperature Effects

An increase in length or volume caused by a rise in temperature is called *thermal expansion.* In your investigations, you found the thermal expansion of air to be much greater than the thermal expansion of solids or liquids. Furthermore, there are differences in thermal expansion between different solids and liquids. For instance, aluminum expands more than an equal length of steel, and alcohol expands more than an equal volume of water.

Rising temperatures cause several other effects on substances, in addition to thermal expansion. At very high temperatures, some objects, including stars, give off light. Depending on how hot an object is, it will give off red, orange, yellow, or white light. The filaments in light bulbs give off bright white light because they reach very high temperatures when electric charges move through them. At lower temperatures, these same filaments have a reddish glow. The ability to give off light at high temperatures is called *incandescence*. That is why ordinary light bulbs are called incandescent bulbs.

A rise or fall in temperature can also cause materials to change their form. Water made cold enough freezes. Water that gets hot enough boils and becomes gaseous steam. Most substances can exist in solid, liquid, or gaseous form if they are cooled or warmed to the right temperatures. Unlike most substances, water expands when it freezes. Such expansion can produce very strong forces.

Temperature also affects the rate or speed of chemical reactions. The most familiar example is cooking food. Food cooks faster at high temperatures. If the temperature is too high, the food will burn. On the other hand, low temperatures preserve food by slowing the chemical reactions that cause food to spoil. Explosions are a dramatic example of how temperature affects a chemical reaction. Dynamite, for example, reacts violently with the oxygen in the air only after its temperature reaches a certain point.

Applications of Thermal Expansion

Thermal expansion has many practical applications. For example, gaps must be placed at regular intervals in sidewalks, roads, bridges, and train tracks so they can expand without buckling and breaking when they get hot. The manufacturers of wagon wheels used to fit the iron rims around the wheel while the rims were still hot. When the rims cooled they shrank and made a very tight fit as shown in Figure 1-5a. Similar methods are used today with steel bolts. Bolts are put in place while hot. Upon cooling, they shrink and pull the pieces they connect tightly together.

In thermostats, two different metals are held together to make what is called a "bimetallic strip." When the strip is heated or cooled, it bends because one metal expands or contracts more than the other. When the temperature is low, the bimetallic strip shown in Figure 1-5b keeps the circuit closed. When the temperature rises, the brass side of the strip expands more than the iron side. This makes the bimetallic strip bend, opening the circuit and turning the heater off.

One of the most practical applications of thermal expansion is used in measuring temperature with a thermometer. By now, you may realize how thermal expansion can be used to measure temperature. As you have seen by observing the water or alcohol level in the liquid expansion device in investigation 1.3, you can tell if the temperature is increasing or decreasing. In the next chapter, you will use this idea to build a thermometer.

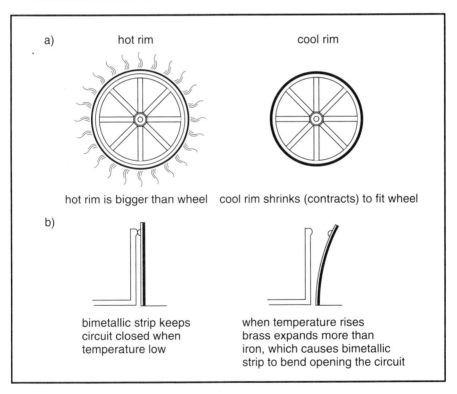

Figure 1-5) Applications of thermal expansion (a) Fitting a rim on a wagon wheel. (b) A simplified bimetallic thermostat switch.

2

Measuring Temperature

One of the most useful scientific instruments is the thermometer, which is based on thermal expansion. In a thermometer, changes in temperature cause changes in length that we can measure objectively. In investigations 2.1 and 2.2 you will use thermal expansion of liquids and gases to build two types of thermometers.

2.1 Building a Liquid Expansion Thermometer

To make a liquid expansion thermometer, rebuild the liquid expansion apparatus used in investigation 1.3. Then place the test tube up to its lip in one of the containers filled with a mixture of crushed ice

Things you'll need:
- materials used in investigation 1–3
- crushed ice or snow
- deep sauce pan

or snow and water. After about 10 minutes, the liquid level in the straw will probably stop moving. Mark this level on the straw with the marking pen.

Transfer the test tube to the other large container filled with the hottest water that comes from the tap. After five minutes, add fresh hot water. After five more minutes, or whenever the liquid level in the straw stops rising, use the pen to mark the new water level on the straw.

The two levels marked on the straw represent two different temperatures. The lower level indicates the temperature of the ice water; the upper level, the temperature of the hot water. If the test tube is placed in warm water, where do you think the liquid level in the straw will lie? Try it. Were you right?

While the test tube is in warm water you can get an idea of how hot or cold the water is. Just compare the level of the liquid in the straw with the levels you found with hot and cold water. For this reason, the ice water and hot water temperatures are called *reference temperatures*.

The measurement of temperature can be made precise by designing a temperature *scale*. Here is how to do it.

(1) Call the temperature of the ice water *0 degrees* (0°). Carefully write it on the cardboard scale next to the ice water mark as shown in Figure 2-1.

(2) Call the temperature of the hot water *10 degrees* (10°), and write it on the cardboard scale next to the hot-water mark.

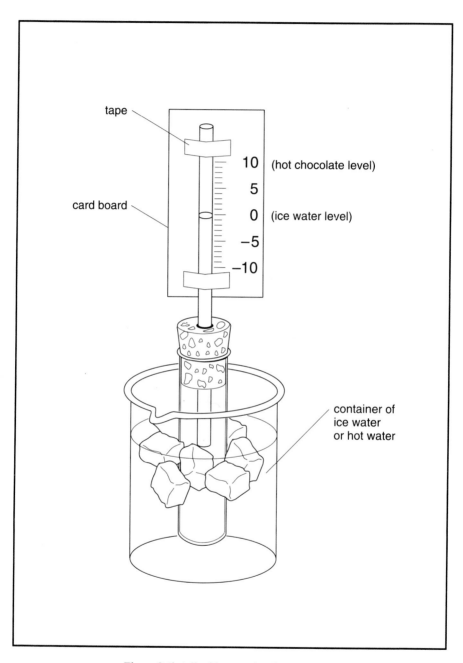

Figure 2-1) A liquid expansion thermometer.

(3) Using the ruler as a guide, divide the distance between the 0° and 10° marks into ten equal lengths. Label these marks 1 through 9.

You have turned the test tube and straw into a temperature measuring instrument or *thermometer*. By assigning numbers to the levels marking the reference temperatures and by dividing the length between these two levels into equal units, you have built a device that can measure different temperatures with some precision.

To extend the temperature scale above 10° and below 0°, mark off equal one degree lengths on the scale. Number the units below 0° with minus signs (-1, -2, -3 . . .).

Use your thermometer to measure the temperature of the room you are in. (Be sure to allow enough time for the apparatus to reach room temperature.)

Can you think of ways to build a thermometer that could measure very cold and very hot temperatures? Why is it important to keep the same amount of colored water in your thermometer? Would your thermometer measure temperature accurately if some of the colored water leaked out?

There is nothing special about calling ice water 0° and hot tap water 10°. Other numbers would serve just as well. It is simply a matter of one's own choosing. Also, the scale marked on the cardboard only applies to this particular thermometer. If a different size test tube or straw or a different amount of colored water were used, a new scale would have to be created by repeating the steps above.

The thermometer you built in this investigation uses water as the temperature-indicating substance. Such a thermometer has two disadvantages. First, it is rather large and clumsy. Second, it takes a long time for the colored water to reach the same temperature as its surroundings. These drawbacks can be overcome by replacing the water with a gas. In the following investigation, you will build a thermometer that uses air as the temperature-indicating substance.

2.2 Building an Air Expansion Thermometer

To build an air thermometer, hold the plastic straw sideways and inject a drop of the colored water into one end with the eye dropper. This will serve as a water plug as in investigation 1–4.

Gently tilt the straw upward and let the water plug slide about 1.5 inches (4 centimeters) down the straw. Without moving the water plug, pinch flat about 3/4 inch (2 centimeters) of the straw at its lower end and fold the end over as shown in Figure 2-2. Wrap the folded end of the straw firmly with the tape.

Things you'll need:

- transparent plastic drinking straw
- water colored with a drop or two of food coloring
- eye dropper
- cellophane tape
- two plastic containers to hold liquids and ice
- crushed ice or snow
- marking pen

Place the straw into one of the containers filled with a mixture of crushed ice (or snow) and water. Observe how the water plug moves. Use the pen to mark the final level reached by the lower end of the water plug.

How much time did it take for the air thermometer to reach the same temperature as the ice water? Is this an advantage compared to the liquid thermometer?

Fill the second container with very hot tap water and insert the straw. Mark the new position reached by the lower end of the water plug.

The two marks on the straw represent the same 0° and 10° temperatures you measured with the liquid expansion thermometer in investigation 2.1. As before, the length between them can be divided into ten equal units or degrees. As long as the water plug is left intact and the straw is not squeezed or split open, the level of the water plug will serve as an accurate measure of temperature. What is the temperature

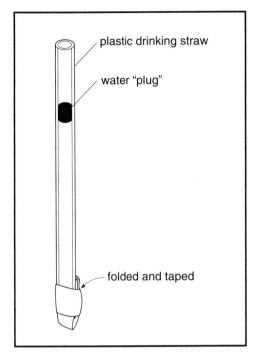

plastic drinking straw

water "plug"

folded and taped

Figure 2-2) An air expansion thermometer.

of the room you are in according to your air thermometer? Does this agree with the room temperature shown by the liquid thermometer you made?

A Brief History of Thermometers

The first thermometer was built in 1593 by Galileo, the famous Italian scientist. It consisted of an inverted glass bulb with a long glass tube that ended in a well of alcohol, as shown in Figure 2-3. As the temperature changed, the air inside the bulb expanded or contracted. This changed the level of the liquid that partially filled the tube.

Galileo left it to others to work out a temperature scale. One person to do so was Sanctorius, a medical doctor who was a friend of Galileo. He chose the temperature of melting snow and of a candle flame as his two reference temperatures.

The first liquid expansion thermometer was built in 1631 by Jean

Rey, a French physician. His thermometer was very similar to the one you built in project 2.1. It consisted of a long, narrow tube connected to the top of a water-filled glass bulb. Rey used his thermometer to detect fevers in his patients.

The next major development in thermometers came with the work of Grand Duke Ferdinand II of Tuscany (Italy) in the years between 1657 and 1667. His thermometers were similar to Rey's, except that they contained alcohol instead of water and the glass tubes were sealed to prevent evaporation. Because alcohol freezes at a lower temperature than water, Ferdinand's thermometers made it possible to measure temperatures lower than the temperature of melting ice. Also, the greater thermal expansion of alcohol made these thermometers more accurate than water thermometers.

Many people tried to come up with a temperature scale that would be widely accepted. Scientists working for Ferdinand chose "the greatest winter cold and the greatest summer heat" as their reference

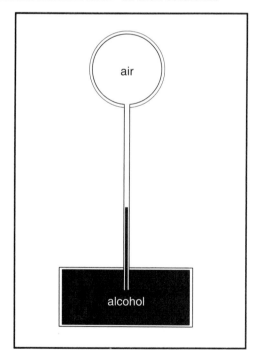

Figure 2-3) Galileo's air thermometer.

28

temperatures. But these temperatures were not the same from year to year and place to place. To solve this problem, Carlo Renaldi, a professor from Padua, Italy, chose the freezing and boiling temperatures of water as reference temperatures. This was a good choice because these temperatures could be easily reproduced and were the same everywhere.

In 1702, René Réaumur, a French physicist, proposed that the temperature of melting ice be made the lower reference point. He assigned it a value of 0° and gave the temperature of boiling water the value of 80°. In 1717, Gabriel Daniel Fahrenheit, a German scientist, proposed the temperature scale still used in the United States. He assigned the value of 32°F to melting ice and 96°F to blood. On this scale, boiling water has a temperature of 212°F.

The centigrade system, which assigns 0°C to the temperature of melting ice and 100°C to the temperature of boiling water, was first suggested in 1710 by Elvius, a Swedish scientist. Credit for this system is often given to Anders Celsius, a Swedish astronomer. Actually, Celsius used Elvius's scale in reverse. That is, he assigned the 100° value to melting ice and 0° to boiling water. In 1948, the centigrade scale was officially named the Celsius scale.

The Celsius and Fahrenheit thermometer scales are the ones most commonly seen in the United States. In Figure 2-4 these two scales appear side-by-side, as they do on many thermometers. You can refer to this figure if you ever need to convert temperatures from one system to the other.

Thermal expansion is not the only effect that can be used to measure temperature. *Pyrometers* measure temperature in terms of the color of light given off by very hot objects. They can measure slight differences in the color of objects that range from red hot to white hot. *Thermistors* and *thermocouples* measure temperature in terms of electrical current which changes with temperature. These devices can be designed to work over a wide range of temperatures. In principle, any property that changes with temperature can be used to make a thermometer.

Just for Fun

- Invent a temperature scale of your own and name it in honor of yourself.

The Common Laboratory Thermometer

The common laboratory thermometer shares many features with the liquid expansion thermometer you built in investigation 2.1. It consists of a hollow glass tube connected to a glass bulb that holds a liquid that can expand or contract. The reference temperatures of melting ice (0°C or 32°F) and boiling water (100°C or 212°F), are scratched onto the glass tube.

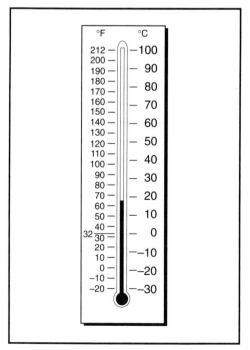

Figure 2-4) The Celsius and Fahrenheit temperature scales on the same thermometer.

30

There are several important differences between the laboratory thermometer and the thermometer you built. First, the laboratory thermometer uses liquid mercury instead of water. Mercury has the advantage of remaining a liquid over a wide range of temperatures (-39°C or -38.2°F to 357°C or 674.6°F). Mercury is easier to see through glass, and it reaches the temperature of its surroundings more rapidly than water. Furthermore, the laboratory thermometer uses a very narrow glass capillary tube instead of a straw, so a temperature change of 1° causes the liquid to move farther when it contracts or expands. A smaller volume of liquid is used in a laboratory thermometer because the expansion is easier to see in the narrow tube. Only a very small change in temperature is required to change the length of so narrow a column of mercury. Lastly, the laboratory thermometer is completely sealed, which prevents the liquid from evaporating.

In the next investigation you will use a laboratory thermometer to measure the temperatures of several objects. You will also discover some interesting temperature effects that you will investigate more thoroughly in Chapter 5.

2.3 Using a Laboratory Thermometer

Use the thermometer to find the temperature near the floor of a room. Be sure to leave the thermometer in place until the temperature reading is steady. Then ask an adult to tape the thermometer to the ceiling so you can measure the temperature near the top of the room. How do the two temperatures compare?

Things you'll need:

- thermometer (-10°C to 110°C)
- tap water
- crushed ice or snow
- insulated coffee cup
- salt
- sauce pan
- a hot plate or stove

Measure the temperature of the coldest and hottest water that comes from the taps in your home or school. **If you are using a household thermometer, remove the thermometer from the water if the liquid in the thermometer gets close to the top end of the scale. Otherwise, you may break the thermometer.**

What is the temperature inside an insulated coffee cup that contains a well-stirred mixture of the crushed ice (or snow) and water? Does the temperature drop any farther if you add more crushed ice or snow? Now add several tablespoonfuls of the salt and remeasure the temperature after stirring for a minute. What do you find? Will the temperature drop any farther if you add more salt?

Ask an adult to help you with the following temperature measurement. Do not attempt to measure the temperature of boiling water unless your thermometer has a scale that goes beyond 100°C (212°F). Boil water in the sauce pan on the hot plate or stove and measure its temperature. Now add a few tablespoonfuls of salt and stir it in. Remeasure the temperature when the water begins to boil again. Does the boiling temperature change when salt is added?

What is the temperature inside a refrigerator? Inside the freezer compartment of the same refrigerator?

Did any of these measurements surprise you? How many degrees hotter is boiling water than the hottest tap water? How many degrees colder is ice water than the coldest tap water? Can you explain why ocean water does not freeze as readily as lake water? Can you explain why it is better to place home furnaces in the basement rather than in the attic?

Exploring on Your Own

- On a sunny day, measure the temperature on the south side of a building. Then measure the temperature on the north side of the same building. What do you find? How can you explain your results? Measure the temperature on the east and west sides of the same building at different times throughout the day. What do you find? Can you explain your results?

- On a spring, summer, or autumn day when a building is not being heated, measure the temperature in a room at ground level. Then predict how the temperature in this room will compare with the temperature in the basement and with the temperature in the attic. If possible, measure these temperatures. Were your predictions correct?

- Measure the temperature on a black-top or asphalt walk on a bright sunny day. Then measure the temperature on a grassy lawn near the walk. How do the temperatures compare? How do they compare with the temperature in a grassy area that is shaded?

- Place a thermometer in each of three identical clear plastic containers. Fill one container with cold water. Add an equal *weight* of sand or soil to the second container. Fill the third container with air. Record the temperature in all three containers. Then put them in a bright sunny place. Record the temperature in all the containers every five minutes. Which container warms up the fastest? Which warms up the slowest? When their temperatures stop rising, bring all three containers into a cool place. Which container cools the fastest? Which container cools the slowest?

Big Temperature Differences

Table 1 lists examples of temperatures of different substances and locations. After reading this table, you might wonder if there is a highest or lowest temperature. It turns out that while there is no highest temperature, there is a lowest temperature. In the next investigation you will use an air thermometer to estimate this lowest temperature.

TABLE 1: TEMPERATURES IN THE UNIVERSE		
	Temperature	
	Celsius (°C)	Fahrenheit (°F)
Inside an exploding star (a supernova)	1,000,000,000	1,800,000,000
Center of the sun	16,000,000	29,000,000
Surface of the sun	6,000	10,800
Light bulb filament	2,600	4,700
Melting iron	1,535	2,795
Candle flame	750	1,380
Water boils	100	212
Normal human body	37.0	98.6
Ice melts	0	32
Grain alcohol freezes	-117	-179
Air becomes a liquid	-196	-321
Surface of Neptune	-220	-360

2.4 The Coldest Temperature*

As you know, an air thermometer uses the thermal expansion of air to measure temperature. When the temperature rises, the air trapped in the thermometer expands and

Things you'll need:

• same as investigation 2.2 plus a laboratory thermometer

pushes the water plug to higher levels. When the temperature decreases, the air contracts and the level of the water plug drops.

There is no limit to the expansion of air. This suggests that there is no upper limit to temperature. On the other hand, air cannot contract below zero volume, which suggests that there is a lowest temperature. To estimate the lowest temperature in degrees Celsius, carry out the following experiment.

(1) Pinch and fold over one end of the drinking straw. Then seal it in place with tape. (See Figure 2-2.)

(2) Fill one of the containers with very hot tap water and insert the laboratory thermometer. Stir the hot water until it reaches 40°C. Then immediately lower the straw into the water until its opened end is just above the surface of the water.

(3) Inject a drop of the colored water into the straw with the eye dropper. It should form a water plug that stays near the top of the straw.

(4) Use the pen to mark the level of the bottom end of the water plug. This indicates the 40°C level on your air thermometer.

(5) Transfer the drinking straw to a container that holds a mixture of crushed ice (or snow) and water. The level of the water plug should quickly drop. After the plug stops moving, mark its new level. This indicates the 0°C level on your air thermometer.

(6) Remove the straw and carefully measure the length between the 40°C and 0°C marks with a ruler. Use this length to mark off a scale of minus temperatures all the way to the bottom of the straw. The reading at the bottom of the straw represents the coldest temperature. Ideally, at this point the volume of air in the straw would be zero. What

is the lowest temperature on your scale? Is it possible to use this air thermometer to measure this temperature? Why or why not?

Absolute Zero

When the experiment in project 2.4 is performed with great care using very precise equipment, the lowest temperature is found to be -273.15°C (-459.67°F). How does this temperature compare with your result? This lowest temperature, called absolute zero, can never be reached. Although scientists have come up with ways to make things extremely cold, no one has been able to get anything all the way down to -273.15°C. However, scientists have managed to reach temperatures within a small fraction of a degree of absolute zero.

You have seen that thermometers can be used to measure temperature and changes in temperature. In Chapter 3, you will try to find patterns or rules that govern the ways temperatures change. Then you will try to devise your own theories to explain the rules of temperature change. Finding and explaining the patterns found in nature is what science is all about. It is what scientists do.

3

A Theory of Temperature Change

When a cold object is put in contact with a hot object, the cold object warms up and the hot object cools down until they reach the same temperature. This is a basic rule of temperature change. It is a rule you have learned from experience. In fact, you count on it working every time you use a stove or refrigerator.

Rules or laws of nature describe patterns found in nature. Discovering these rules is a basic goal of scientists. Another goal is to explain these rules. To know them is not enough. Scientists are driven to understand *why* and *how* the laws of nature work as they do.

An explanation of a rule of nature is called a *theory*. For a theory to be any good, it must explain a particular rule without contradicting any other rule. The best theories explain many rules of nature and even predict new ones. In this chapter you will carry out investigations that can help you discover additional rules of temperature change and build a theory to explain temperature change.

3.1 Two More Rules of Temperature Change

To begin, fill the 48-oz can about half full with cold tap water. Add ice cubes until the can is about two-thirds full. Gently stir the mixture of ice and water with the thermometer until the temperature of the mixture is close to 0°C. Then remove the unmelted ice.

Next, add hot tap water to the 96-oz can or sauce pan until it is about one-third full. Use the thermometer to measure the temperature

Things you'll need:

- 48-oz metal can
- tap water
- ice cubes
- thermometer (-10°C to 110°C)
- 96-oz metal can or 3-quart or larger sauce pan
- 16-oz metal can
- clock or watch with a second hand

in both cans. Record both temperatures in your notebook. Immediately after you have measured the two temperatures, place the can with cold water into the can with hot water as shown in Figure 3-1.

Measure the temperatures of the cold and hot water every minute until no further change occurs. Gently swirl the water in the smaller can between measurements. Make a table like Table 2 in your notebook. Record the temperatures in it. (Do not write in this book.)

When did the two water temperatures change at the fastest rate? When did they change more slowly? Does the rate or speed of temperature change depend on the difference in temperature between the cold and the hot water? Write a rule that describes what you have observed.

How did the final temperature reached by the cold water compare with the final temperature reached by the hot water? Write a rule that describes this discovery.

Repeat the experiment using the 16-oz can for the cold water. Do the rules you discovered in the first experiment still hold true in this experiment? How do the final temperatures in this experiment compare with the ones you measured when you used a larger amount of cold water?

When the 16-oz can is used, a smaller amount of cold water is being warmed by the same amount of hot water as used for the 48-oz can. The result is a higher final temperature for both. This means that the temperature of the cold water has increased by a greater amount than the temperature of the hot water has decreased. Can you write a rule that describes how temperature change depends on the amounts of hot and cold water used?

Imagine performing the same two experiments with hot water in the inner can and cold water in the outer can. Can you predict what the final temperatures will be? Try the experiment. Were your predictions right?

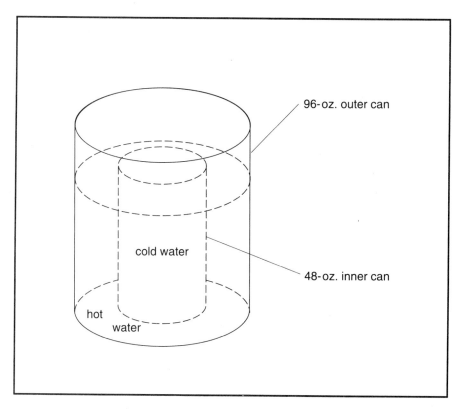

Figure 3-1) Searching for rules of temperature change.

	Temperature (°C)	
TABLE 2: TEMPERATURE AND TIME DATA FOR INVESTIGATION 3.1		
Time (minutes)	**Outer can (hot water)**	**Inner can (cold water)**
start		
1		
2		
3		
4		
5		
6		
. . .		

Exploring on Your Own

- Use a thermometer to measure the temperature of a bucket of cold tap water. Then add an eye dropperful of hot tap water to the bucket. Can you detect any temperature change in the bucket?

The Rules of Temperature Change

Investigation 3.1 revealed two more rules of temperature change. Were you able to find them? All three rules are listed below. See if they are similar to the rules you wrote.

(1) When objects with different temperatures are put in contact, the cooler one gets warmer and the warmer one gets cooler until their temperatures are equal.

(2) The greater the difference in temperature between two touching objects, the faster their temperatures change.

(3) The greater the amount of something, the greater the tempera-

ture change it can cause in another object, and the less its own temperature changes in the process.

These rules have some important consequences. Rule 1 tells us that objects can only get as hot or as cold as the other objects they are in contact with. For instance, an egg in boiling water will never get hotter than the water. Rule 1 also explains how it is possible to measure temperatures. A thermometer will reach the same temperature as the object it is measuring.

Rule 3 also plays an important role in temperature measurement. It tells us that a cold thermometer placed in hot water will cool the water by a small amount. The larger the thermometer, the more it will lower the water's temperature. If we do not want a thermometer to change the temperature of the object it is measuring, it must be much smaller than the object.

Exploring on Your Own

- Pour a cup of tap water into a container and measure the temperature of the water. Remove an ice cube from a freezer. How does the temperature of the ice compare with the temperature of the water? Place the ice cube in the water and stir until all the ice is melted. How do the temperatures of the water and the melted ice compare now?

- Place a cup of tap water in a container. Place 2 cups of water in a second container. In a third, place 4 cups of water. Put identical ice cubes into each container. Which ice cube melts the fastest? Which ice cube melts the slowest? In which container is the temperature highest after all the ice has melted? How can you explain your results?

- Place identical ice cubes in each of two containers. Add a cup of cold tap water to one container. Add a cup of hot tap water to the other. In which container does the ice melt faster? Why?

Graphing Temperature Change

In investigation 3.1, you discovered three rules for temperature change. A useful way of showing how these rules work is to make a *graph* of the temperature and time data you collected.

When the authors performed the first part of experiment 3.1, they obtained the data shown in Table 3. Your data should be similar. Their numbers are plotted as points on the *temperature versus time* graph shown in Figure 3-2. The line for the vertical scale is the *temperature axis*. The line for the horizontal scale is the *time axis*.

The points on the graph are connected by a smooth line. This allows you to predict temperatures in between the times the measurements were actually taken. For example, the temperature of the cold

TABLE 3: AUTHORS' TEMPERATURE VERSUS TIME DATA FOR INVESTIGATION 3.1		
	Temperature (°C)	
Time (minutes)	Outer can (hot water)	Inner can (cold water)
0 (start)	52	0
0.5	44	8
1.0	38	15
1.5	34	20
2.0	31	23
2.5	30	24
3.0	39	35
3.5	28	25
4.0	27	26
4.5	27	27
5.0	27	27

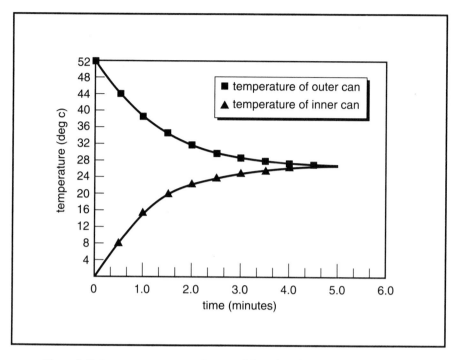

Figure 3-2) A temperature versus time graph based on data obtained by authors.

water at 1.25 minutes can be estimated from the graph to be 17°C. The temperature of the hot water at this same time was about 36°C.

By connecting the points with a smooth line we make an *educated guess* about what happened in between our measurements. We *assume* that the temperature did not make any quick jumps between the measured times. To be more certain about what really happened, it would have been necessary to watch the thermometer continually, or to make more frequent measurements.

An upward-sloping line on this graph means that temperature was increasing. A downward-sloping line means that the temperature was decreasing. The steepness of the sloping lines shows how fast the temperature increased or decreased. The steeper the line, the faster the temperature changed. A flat or horizontal line means that the temperature was constant.

The graph clearly illustrates the first and second rules of temperature change. It shows that the temperature of the cold water increased and the temperature of the warm water decreased until they reached the same temperature. It also shows that the rate of temperature change was greatest in the beginning of the experiment when the temperature difference was greatest. The rate of temperature change gradually slowed down as the hot and cold water approached the same temperature.

Draw your own temperature versus time graphs using the data you obtained in project 3.1. Make a graph for both parts of the experiment. Examine the graphs carefully. Can you see how they show all three rules of temperature change?

A Process Similar to Temperature Change

How do we explain the three rules of temperature change? That is, how can we come up with a theory of temperature change? One way might be to find a different process that follows similar rules. We could then explain temperature change by saying it is *like* this other process.

Explaining one thing by comparing it with another is a common practice in science. For example, an early theory of light compared its behavior with that of water waves. More recently, some scientists have attempted to understand the human brain by comparing it with a computer.

In the following investigation you will see that the behavior of water flowing between connected containers is very similar to the process of temperature change. This investigation will provide the key for building your theory.

3.2 Fluid Level Changes in Connected Containers

We will try to explain the three rules of temperature change by observing how the water levels in two buckets change as the water flows from one to the other.

(1) **Ask an adult to help you use the finishing nail or metal compass point to make a small hole in the side of each of the two plastic buckets.** Make the holes 0.75 in (2 cm) from the bottom of each bucket. Punch a similar hole in the bottle or cup.

(2) Enlarge the holes by gently twisting and pushing the sharpened pencil into them. Make the holes the same size as the plastic drinking straws you will use to connect the buckets.

Things you'll need:

- finishing nail or metal compass point

- two large 5–quart or larger plastic buckets with straight sides

- tall, narrow plastic bottle or cup with straight sides

- sharpened pencil

- several plastic drinking straws

- tape

- scissors

- petroleum jelly

- water

- clock or watch with a second hand

(3) Use the scissors to cut off three strips of tape. Make a vertical depth scale (in centimeters) on each strip and stick one scale on the outside of each container. Start the scale at the top of each hole and label this first mark 0 cm. Label the two buckets #1 and #2. (See Figure 3-3.)

(4) Coat both ends of one of the drinking straws with some of the petroleum jelly. Then connect buckets #1 and #2 by inserting the ends of the straw into the holes. Be sure that the jelly does not clog the straw.

(5) Fill bucket #2 with water up to the 0 cm level. Then, while pinching the plastic straw closed, fill bucket #1 to the 10-cm mark.

(6) Release the straw and begin timing with the clock or watch.

As the water flows from bucket #1 into bucket #2, measure the two water levels on the scales of each bucket every 30 seconds. This may require three people: one to call out the time at 30-second intervals and two to measure the water level in each bucket.

(7) Record the results in your notebook in a table like Table 4. Then draw a *water level versus time graph*, as shown in Figure 3-4.

Look at your graph. How does it compare with the one the authors

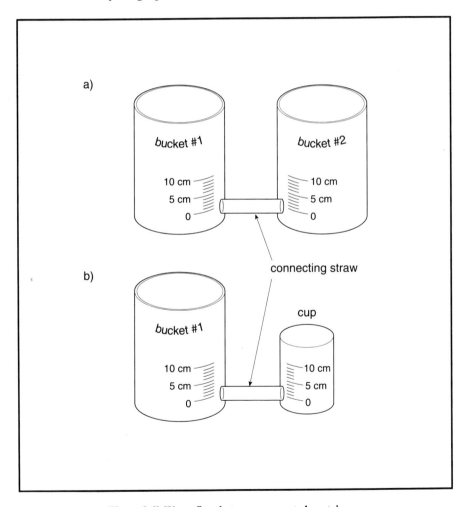

Figure 3-3) Water flow between connected containers.

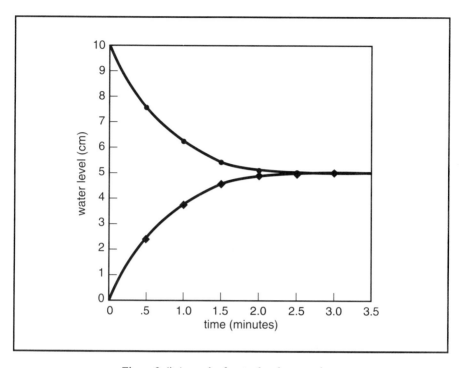

Figure 3-4) A graph of water level versus time.

made in Figure 3-4? When did the water levels change at the fastest rate? When did the water levels change at the slowest rate? How does the rate at which the water levels change depend on the difference in levels between the two buckets? Can you write a rule that describes this behavior?

How does the final water level in bucket #1 compare with the final level in bucket #2? Can you write a rule that describes this result?

Repeat the above experiment using the narrow plastic bottle in place of bucket #2 as shown in Figure 3-3b. Record your results in a new table and a new graph.

Are the final water levels in the narrow bottle and larger bucket equal? How do these final levels compare to those reached when two identical buckets were used? Can you write a rule that describes how

TABLE 4: WATER DEPTH VERSUS TIME FOR TWO BUCKETS		
	Water depth (cm)	
Time (minutes)	Bucket #1	Bucket #2
0	10	0
0.5		
1.0		
1.5		
2.0		
2.5		
3.0		
. . .		

changes in water levels depend on the size of the connected containers?

Imagine performing the above experiment with the water flowing from a height of 10 cm in the narrow bottle into the larger bucket. Can you predict what the final water levels will be? Try the experiment. Are your results close to your prediction?

Exploring on Your Own

- You can perform the experiments described in investigation 3.2 in a different way. Instead of using a straw to connect the buckets or the bucket and the narrow bottle, use a *siphon*—a narrow length of flexible plastic or rubber tubing—to allow water to flow from one vessel to the other.

- Get two new buckets. Start with one bucket filled with water and the other one empty. Coil the entire length of tubing so it rests beneath the surface of the water in the full bucket. The tubing should fill with water. Squeeze both ends of the tubing tightly. Keep one end at the bottom of the full bucket. Lift the other end and place it at the bottom of the empty bucket. Then release the ends of the tubing. You will see water flow from the full bucket to the empty one as shown in Figure 3-5. When does the water stop flowing? Does its rate of flow change as the water level in the full bucket falls?

• Now perform the experiment again. This time, use the narrow bottle and one bucket. Are the results similar to what you found when the containers were connected by a straw?

How Fluid Levels Change

Based on the results of investigation 3.2, the rules of changing fluid levels may be written as follows.

(1) When containers with different fluid levels are connected, the

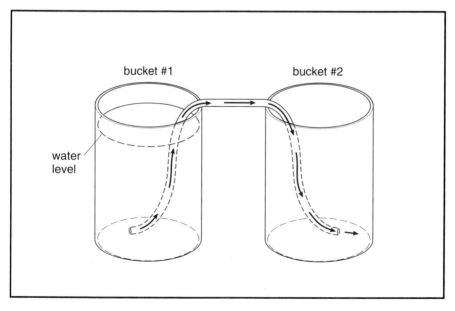

Figure 3-5) A siphon can be used in place of a straw connector. Arrows show direction of water flow.

lower level rises and the higher level drops until they are both at the same level.

(2) The greater the difference in fluid levels between two connected containers, the faster their levels change.

(3) The greater the volume of a container, the greater the change in fluid level it can cause in another container, and the less its own level changes in the process.

Fluid levels drop because of gravity. Just as solid objects fall until they hit the ground, so fluids flow to the lowest possible level. When fluid flows between connected containers, the fluid level in one rises and the level in the other falls. When the two levels become equal, there is no lower place for the fluid to flow, and no further change takes place.

Building a Theory of Temperature Change

If you compare the rules of fluid level change with those of temperature change, you will find striking similarities. In fact, you could turn one set of rules into the other set by simply switching a few words. This is best seen by placing the rules side by side.

Rules of Temperature Change

(1) When objects having different temperatures are put in contact, the cooler one gets warmer and the warmer one gets cooler until their temperatures become equal.

(2) The greater the difference in temperature between two touching objects, the faster their temperatures change.

(3) The greater the amount of something, the greater the temperature change it can cause in another object, and the less its own temperature changes.

Rules of Fluid Level Change

(1) When containers having different fluid levels are connected, the lower level rises and the higher level drops until their levels become equal.

(2) The greater the difference in fluid levels between two connected containers, the faster their fluid levels change.

(3) The greater the volume of a container, the greater the change in fluid level it can cause in another container, and the less its own level changes in the process.

The similarities in the results of experiments 3.1 and 3.2 can be used to build a theory of temperature change. The first step is to see that changes in temperature are *like* changes in fluid level. Since changes in fluid level are caused by the flow of fluid, we might reason that changes in temperature are caused by the flow of a different type of fluid. We might call this fluid *heat*. The greater the amount of heat given to or taken from an object, the greater its temperature change. Can you explain the three rules of temperature change by showing how they depend on the flow of heat?

We have no proof that heat fluid is like a real fluid. In fact, if it is real, it would have some rather strange properties. First, it would be invisible. Second, it would be able to pass right through the walls of solid metal containers. Third, it could only exist inside other substances. It could not exist by itself. Therefore, we can only *guess* that there might be a heat fluid. Such guesses about the nature of things are called *hypotheses*. Hypotheses are the starting points on which theories are built.

Joseph Black and the Fluid Theory of Heat

It is easy to imagine that temperature changes are caused by the flow of a fluid we call heat. For instance, we commonly say that heat *escapes* from open windows or that pans *absorb* heat from hot stoves.

51

It does seem as if there is some kind of "stuff" that things lose when they cool down and gain when they heat up.

But just what kind of "stuff" is heat? What are its properties? Why does it flow from a hotter object to a colder one? Does heat have weight? How can it be measured? These important questions must be answered before a fluid theory of heat can be taken seriously.

The idea of a heat fluid dates back to the ancient Greek philosophers. However, their ideas were mostly ignored until a few scientists revived them in the early 1700s, when Joseph Black, a Scottish chemist, finally developed a complete fluid theory of heat. Black outlined the properties of heat and showed how it could be measured.

According to Black's theory, heat is made up of very small particles of fluid that cannot be created or destroyed. In this sense, heat is like normal matter. But unlike normal matter, heat particles have no mass or weight.* They are so small that they can fill the spaces between the particles of normal matter and can move through them. Black believed that heat particles are attracted to normal matter and are repelled by each other.

Based on Black's theory, *temperature is a measure of the level of heat in an object.* As more heat enters an object, its temperature increases, just as adding fluid to a container raises its fluid level. Removing heat from an object lowers its temperature, just as removing fluid from a container lowers its fluid level.

Because temperature measures the level of heat and not the total amount of heat, a large cold object may actually have more heat in it than a small hot object, just as a wide container filled to a shallow level can have more fluid in it than a narrow container filled to its brim. (See

---

* The amount of matter in an object is called its mass. The more mass an object has, the more it weighs. An object's mass does not change, but its weight may. For example, you would weigh less on the Moon than you do on Earth, but your mass—the amount of matter in your body—does not change. In this book we will use mass to describe the amount of matter in objects. We will use *grams* as the unit to measure mass.

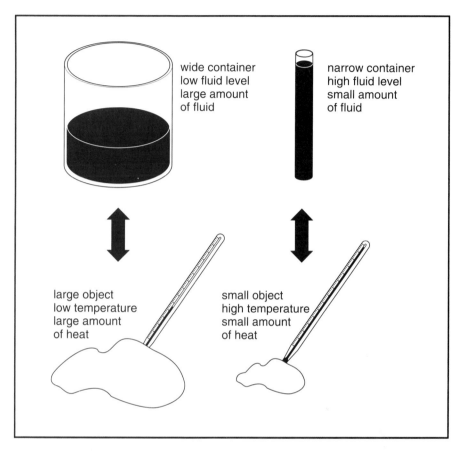

wide container
low fluid level
large amount
of fluid

narrow container
high fluid level
small amount
of fluid

large object
low temperature
large amount
of heat

small object
high temperature
small amount
of heat

Figure 3-6) A large container with a low fluid level can hold more fluid than a small container filled to the brim.

Figure 3-6). This also explains why a large object can cause a large temperature change in a small object while its own temperature changes very little (rule 3).

The idea that temperature is a measure of the level of heat fluid also suggests that temperature changes are *proportional* to the amount of heat added or subtracted. This means that doubling the amount of heat added to an object doubles the temperature change; tripling the amount of heat added triples the temperature change; and so on. To test this idea the authors did the experiment shown in Figure 3-7. An electric immersion heater, such as the kind used to heat water to make a cup of tea, was placed, in turn, in each of three insulated cups. Each cup contained 100 mL of water at 10°C.

In the first cup (Figure 3-7a), the heater was plugged into a wall outlet for 30 seconds. In the second cup (Figure 3-7b), the heater was plugged in for 60 seconds in order to provide twice as much heat. In the third cup (Figure 3-7c), the heater was plugged in for 90 seconds to provide three times as much heat. As you can see from the temperatures and temperature changes shown in Figure 3-7, doubling the heat added does double the temperature change; tripling the heat added does triple the change in temperature.

Black's theory also explained what happens when a hot object is placed in contact with a cool one. The hot object cools down and the cool object warms up (rule 1). According to Black, this happens

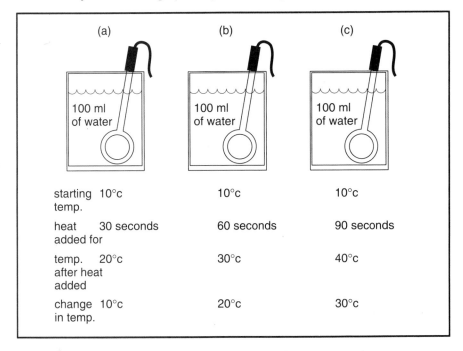

Figure 3-7) The more heat added, the greater the temperature change.

54

because heat particles are attracted to matter but repelled by each other. As a result, they flow from hot regions where they are abundant to cold regions where there is matter but few heat particles.

The idea that heat is attracted to normal matter and repelled by itself also explains why large temperature differences cause rapid temperature change (rule 2). A large difference in temperature means a large difference in heat levels. This causes a rapid flow of heat just as a large difference in fluid levels causes a rapid flow of fluid.

Finally, Black's theory can also explain thermal expansion. When heat fluid enters the spaces between the particles of normal matter, it pushes the particles apart. This leads to an overall expansion just as water soaking into the pores of a dry sponge makes it expand.

The one part of his theory that made Black uncomfortable was the idea that heat is weightless. It is hard to imagine a real substance with no weight. But all attempts to detect the weight of heat failed. Black saw this as a serious problem for his theory. Ultimately, he accepted the fact that his theory was imperfect and hoped that future scientists would improve it or even find a better theory.

The ability to see and admit shortcomings in theories is essential for scientific progress. When a theory is mistaken for the absolute truth, the development of new ideas and better theories is often hindered. This has happened many times in science. The fluid theory of heat is no exception. Scientists were so impressed with Black's theory that they accepted heat as a real but invisible fluid. It took more than a 100 years for a better theory to be accepted. How this came about will be described in later chapters.

Scientists always feel more confident about the existence of something if they can measure it. Joseph Black had the same feeling about heat. In Chapter 4 you will look for a way to measure heat.

4

Measuring Heat

You measure length with a ruler, volume with a graduated cylinder or measuring cup, mass with a balance, time with a clock or watch, and temperature with a thermometer. But how do you measure heat? Joseph Black realized that his theory of heat would be accepted by other scientists only if heat could be measured.

Like you, Black realized that he could not measure heat with a ruler, a balance, or even a thermometer. A rise in an object's temperature indicated that heat was flowing into it, but it did not tell how much heat had been added. If the object were large, it might take a lot of heat to raise its temperature one degree. If it were small, a little heat might raise its temperature a lot. Black realized that measuring heat involved the mass of the material, the kind of material, and its change in temperature.

In the next investigation you will see how both mass and temperature change are involved in measuring heat. First you will investigate how the temperature of a fixed amount of water changes when different amounts of heat are added. Then you will investigate how changing the amount of water affects the temperature change when a fixed amount of heat is added.

4.1 Temperature Changes and Heat*

In this investigation you will be using matches and a flame. Ask an adult to help you. You know from experience that a candle flame gives off heat. The longer it burns, the more heat it gives off. If a candle burns evenly, it is reasonable to assume that during equal periods of time it gives off equal amounts of heat.

Call the amount of heat given off by a single candle flame during a 1–minute period 1 dose of heat. This means that the same candle gives off 2 doses of heat in 2 minutes, 3 doses of heat in 3 minutes, and so on.

Using Figure 4-1a as a guide, follow the steps listed below to build a heat–measuring device.

Things you'll need:

- piece of modeling clay
- package of birthday candles
- ring stand to hold juice can; alternatively, aluminum foil, or a large can, a can opener, and a stick
- 6-oz frozen juice can with metal bottom and cardboard sides
- 100 mL graduated cylinder or a measuring cup
- laboratory thermometer
- paper towels
- clock or watch with a second hand.

(1) Mold a simple candleholder from the clay. Insert one of the candles upright in the holder and place it under the ring stand. Adjust the candle's height until the tip of its wick is about 0.2 in (0.5 cm) below the bottom of the juice can. Then slide the ringstand away from the candle.

If you do not have a ringstand, you can fold a piece of aluminum foil into a V-shaped stand (Figure 4-1b). Or you can use a large can and a stick to support the small can as shown in Figure 4-1c. By resting the stick on the top rim of the big can, you can support the small can above the candle. Use a can opener to make 4 or 5 openings along the bottom of the can so air can get to the candle. Use melted wax from

57

the candle to fasten it to a lid from a small can. Then place the large can over the candle.

(2) Measure 100 mL of cool tap water with the graduated cylinder and pour it into the juice can. Since 1 mL of water has a mass of 1 gram (g), 100 mL of water has a mass of 100 g. Thus, a graduated cylinder can be used to measure out a mass of water. This is a lot faster than using a balance.

(3) Set the can on the ring stand (or alternative stand) and use the thermometer to measure the water's initial (starting) temperature. Record this temperature in a table in your notebook. The table below can serve as a model. (Do not write in this book.)

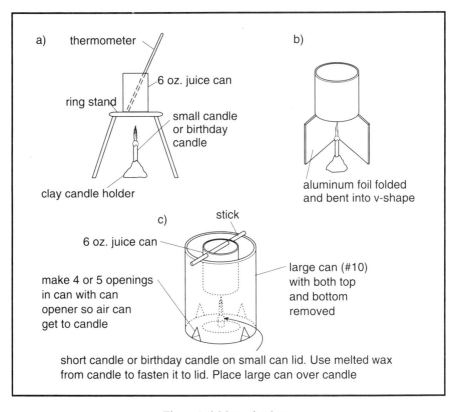

Figure 4-1) Measuring heat.

TABLE FOR 4–1				
Amount of water (grams)	Heating Time (minutes)	Initial Temp (°C)	Final Temp (°C)	Change in Temp (°C)
100	1 (= 1 dose)			
100	2 (= 2 doses)			
100	3 (= 3 doses)			
50	1 (= 1 dose)			
150	1 (= 1 dose)			
50	2 (= 2 doses)			
150	2 (= 2 doses)			

(4) **With an adult present**, light the candle and slide the juice can directly over the flame. Gently stir the water with the thermometer as it is heating. After the water has been heated for 1 minute (measured with the clock or watch), blow out the candle and continue stirring the water for a few seconds. Then measure the final temperature of the water. How can you calculate the water's change in temperature? Write down both the final temperature and the change in temperature in your table.

(5) Empty the water from the can and wipe the soot off the bottom with a wet paper towel.

(6) Follow the same procedure to heat a fresh 100-g (100 mL) sample of cool water for 2 minutes. Then, heat a third 100-g sample of cool water for 3 minutes. Be sure to adjust the candle holder at the start of each test so the wick is always the same distance below the can.

When you double the amount of heat added to the water, does the temperature change of the water just about double too? If you triple the amount of heat added, does the temperature change of the water also just about triple? Would you have predicted these results using the fluid theory of heat?

So far, you have measured temperature changes when different amounts of heat are added to the same amount of water. To find out what happens when a fixed amount of heat is added to *different* amounts of water, add 1 dose of heat to 50 g (50 mL) of water, and then add 1 dose of heat to 150 g (150 mL) of water. Finally, add 2 doses of heat to 50 g of water and then to 150 g of water.

Based on your complete table, how does doubling the mass of water affect the temperature change when a fixed amount of heat is added? How does tripling the amount of water affect the temperature change when a fixed amount of heat is added? Can the fluid theory of heat explain these results?

A careful review of investigation 4.1 reveals two new rules of temperature change in addition to the three we found earlier.

(Rule 4) The increase in temperature of a fixed amount of water is *directly proportional* to the amount of heat added. (Directly proportional means that two quantities or measurements increase or decrease together at the same rate. Doubling the amount of heat doubles the temperature increase. Likewise, tripling the amount of heat triples the temperature increase, and so on.)

(Rule 5) When a constant amount of heat is added to a substance, its increase in temperature is *inversely proportional* to its mass. (Inversely proportional means that increasing one quantity *decreases* the other at the same rate. In this experiment, if a constant amount of heat is added, doubling the mass reduces the temperature increase by half. Likewise, tripling the mass reduces the temperature increase to one-third, and so on.)

Measuring Heat: The Calorie

When the authors performed project 4.1, they obtained the results shown in Table 5. Notice that Table 5 has a new column at the right. This column shows the number obtained when the mass of the water (in grams) is multiplied by its change in temperature (in degrees

TABLE 5: AUTHORS' RESULTS FOR INVESTIGATION 4–1

Amount of water	Heating Time (minutes)	Initial Temp (°C)	Final Temp (°C)	Change in °C Temp	Amount of water x Temp change (calorie)
100	1 (= 1 dose)	20.0	25.0	5.0	500
100	2 (= 2 doses)	19.5	29.5	10.0	1,000
100	3 (= 3 doses)	19.5	34.1	14.6	1,460
50	1 (= 1 dose)	19.7	29.7	10.0	500
150	1 (= 1 dose)	19.7	23.0	3.3	495
50	2 (= 2 doses)	19.6	38.7	19.1	955
150	2 (= 2 doses)	19.6	26.7	7.1	1,065

Celsius). Notice that when 1 dose of heat is added to the water, the product (mass x temperature change) is always about 500, no matter how much water is used. When 2 doses of heat are added, the product is always about 1,000 or 2 x 500. When 3 doses of heat are added, the product is 1,450, which is close to 1,500 or 3 x 500. No matter what the temperature change is, or the mass of water, this product, in multiples of 500, always shows how many doses of heat were added.

So, the product of the mass of the water and the temperature change can be used to measure heat. When this method is used the unit of heat is called the *calorie*:

Heat (in calories) = **mass of water** (in grams) x **temperature change** (in °C)

This equation defines 1 calorie (cal) as the amount of heat needed to raise the temperature of 1 gram of water by 1°C. If the temperature of 1 g of water increases by 1°C, 1 calorie of heat has been added to the water. If the temperature of 100 g of water rises by 5°C, 500 calories of heat have been added. In our experiment, the candles we used released about 500 calories per minute. In other words, 1 dose of heat in our experiment was equal to 500 calories. How many calories of heat were in 1 dose of your candle flame?

Exploring on Your Own

- With an adult present, use the equipment you used in investigation 4.1 to measure the amount of heat, in calories, released *per gram* of candle wax for several different kinds of candles.

Big Calories and Food

You have probably heard people talk about calories when they are dieting. The calorie involved in diets is 1,000 times bigger than the calorie you learned about in the last section. A big calorie, a Calorie (Cal) with a capital "C," is the amount of heat it takes to raise the temperature of 1,000 g or 1 kilogram (kg) of water 1°C.

The heat content of various foods can actually be measured by burning the food in a closed container, called a bomb calorimeter.

The food is placed in the center of the container and burned in oxygen. The heat produced flows into cold water in a jacket that surrounds the food. Experiments show that when one gram of sugar burns, 4.5 Calories (4,500 calories) are produced.

If the jacket around a bomb calorimeter contains 1 kg of water, by how much will its temperature rise if a 10 g piece of candy is burned in the calorimeter? (Assume the candy is all sugar.)

Conservation of Heat

According to Joseph Black's theory, heat is made up of particles that cannot be created or destroyed. Another way of saying this is that *heat is conserved*; that is, the total amount of heat never changes. If heat is conserved, then whenever one object loses heat, all the heat lost must be absorbed by another object (or objects). In the following investigation, you will test the idea that heat is conserved.

4.2 Is Heat Conserved When Hot and Cold Water Are Mixed?*

You know from experience that insulated cups keep hot drinks hot and cold drinks cold for some time. You might say that insulation slows the rate at which heat can "leak" out of the cup or into the cup from the outside.

Even though Styrofoam and other insulators do not stop the flow of heat completely, over short periods of time very little heat gets

Things you'll need:

• two or three insulated cups
• container
• 100 mL graduated cylinder or a measuring cup
• two laboratory thermometers
• hot and cold tap water
• ice

through them. Therefore, if we *rapidly* mix two quantities of water at different temperatures in an insulated cup, most of the heat will stay in the cup. Also, if heat is neither created nor destroyed, then any heat lost by the warmer water should be absorbed by the cooler water. To see if this actually happens, carry out the following experiment.

(1) Use the graduated cylinder or measuring cup to measure out 75 mL of cold water that has a temperature close to 0°C. (To prepare such water, mix the water with the ice in the container. But make sure that no small pieces of ice are in the water when it is added to the cup.) Pour the water into one of the insulated cups.

(2) Fill the second cup with 75 mL of hot water from the tap.

(3) Measure the water temperatures in each cup and record them in your notebook in a table like the one shown below. If you have only one thermometer, measure the temperature of the cold water first. Then cover the cup of cold water with another cup while you measure the temperature of the hot water.

(4) Immediately pour the hot water into the cold water. Stir the mixture with the thermometer for about 10 seconds and measure the

final temperature. Record the result in your notebook in a table like the Data Table 4-2.

DATA TABLE 4–2				
Hot water		Cold Water		
Mass	Starting temp	Mass (g)	Starting temp	Mixture final temp
75 g	°C	75 g	°C	°C
100 g	°C	50 g	°C	°C
50 g	°C	100 g	°C	°C

(5) Calculate the amount of heat *gained* by the cool water during the mixing process. Use the equation:

Heat (in calories) = **mass of water** (in grams) x **temperature change** (in °C)

(6) Now calculate the amount of heat, in calories, *lost* by the warm water during the mixing process. Use the same equation and assume that a gram of water loses as much heat in cooling one degree as it gains when its temperature rises one degree.

How did the amount of heat lost by the warm water compare with the amount of heat gained by the cold water?

(7) Repeat the experiment using 100 g of hot water and 50 g of cold water. Again, calculate the heat gained by the cold water and the heat lost by the hot water.

Was heat conserved in this experiment? What effect would waiting a long time before measuring the temperatures have on the results?

(8) Try to predict the final temperature of a mixture of 50 g of hot water and 100 g of cold water. Test your prediction by performing the experiment.

Heating Different Substances

You have learned that it takes 1 calorie of heat to raise the temperature of 1 g of water by 1°C. Does it also take 1 calorie to raise the temperature of 1 g of another substance by 1°C? You can explore this question by seeing how the temperature of cooking oil changes when heat is added.

4.3 Temperature Changes in Cooking Oil

To begin, make a table in your notebook like Table 6. To the 6-oz frozen juice can add 50 g (50 mL) of tap water and measure its initial temperature. Record the temperature in your table.

Things you'll need:

- same materials used in investigation 4.1
- water
- about 8 oz of cooking oil

Be careful of the flame from the candle. With an adult present, heat the water with a candle for exactly one minute just as you did in project 4.1. Measure the final temperature of the water after stirring. Then calculate the change in temperature. Enter both values in your table.

Using the equation for heat, calculate the amount of heat the candle added to the water in 1 minute. It should be almost the same as the value you found in investigation 4.1.

Now add 56 mL of cooking oil to an empty juice can. This amount of oil has a mass of 50 grams.

Measure the initial temperature of the cool cooking oil and record it in your table. **Then ask an adult to help you heat the cooking oil** over the candle flame for exactly 1 minute. Stir the oil, measure its final temperature, and calculate the change in temperature of the cooking oil. Record the values in your table.

TABLE 6 (PROJECT 4.3)		
	Water	**Cooking Oil**
Mass (grams)	50	50
Initial Temp (°C)		
Final Temp (°C)		
Temperature change (°C)		
Heat gained (calories)		

Since the oil was heated for the *same time* with the same candle, it must have received the *same amount of heat* as the water. Record, in your table, the heat added to the cooking oil.

How does the temperature increase of the cooking oil compare with that of the water? For the same mass, which substance requires more heat to raise its temperature 1°C? How many calories of heat are required to raise the temperature of 50 g (56 mL) of cooking oil by just 1°C? How many calories are required to raise the temperature of just 1 gram of cooking oil by 1°C?

When the authors performed the above experiment, they obtained the results shown in Table 7. They found that the temperature change of the cooking oil was about twice as much as the water's when the same amount of heat was added to each. It must take about twice as much heat to raise the temperature of 50 g of water by 1°C as it does to raise the temperature of the same amount of cooking oil 1 degree.

Exploring on Your Own

- Suppose you mix 56 mL (50 g) of cold cooking oil with 50 mL (50 g) of hot tap water and stir the mixture thoroughly. Do you think the new temperature of the mixture will be halfway between the two initial temperatures as it is for hot and cold water? Measure the temperature of 56 mL (50 g) of cold cooking oil and 50 mL (50 g)

TABLE 7: AUTHOR'S RESULTS FOR PROJECT 4.3	Water	Cooking Oil
Mass (grams)	50	50
Initial Temp (°C)	18.5	19.0
Final Temp (°C)	28.5	38.5
Temperature change (°C)	10.0	19.5
Heat gained (calories)	500	500

of hot tap water, both in insulated cups. See if you can predict the temperature you will get when you mix the two. How close did you come?

- Repeat the experiment starting with *cold* water and *warm* cooking oil. You can cool the water by placing it in a refrigerator. Warm the oil by putting the bottle in a large pan of hot tap water for about 10 minutes. **Do not try to heat the oil on a stove or with a flame. It might catch fire, burn, or spatter**. Can you predict the final temperature of a mixture of cold water and warm cooking oil?

Just for Fun

- Watch an ice cube melt in room temperature cooking oil. You'll enjoy seeing beautiful round drops of water that form and sink to the bottom of the oil.

Heat Capacity

As you have seen, when the same amount of heat is added to equal masses of cooking oil and water, the change in temperature of the oil is about twice as much as the change in temperature of the water. This means that it takes less heat to change the temperature of 1 g of cooking oil by 1°C than it does to change the temperature of 1 g of water by

1°C. For example, if you used an immersion heater for 30 seconds to warm 100 g of water from 20°C to 30°C, you know that the heater added 1,000 cal of heat to the water. (100 g x 10°C = 1,000 calories) If you used the same heater for 30 seconds to warm 100 g of cooking oil initially at 20°C, you would find its final temperature to be about 40°C. So, 1,000 calories of heat raised the temperature of the 100 g of cooking oil 20°C. Raising the temperature of 1 g of cooking oil by 1°C requires only 0.5 calories.

If we divide the heat absorbed by an object by its temperature change, the value we get tells us how much heat is required to raise the object's temperature by 1°C. If it takes 1,000 calories to raise the temperature of a certain object 10°C, it will only take 100 calories to raise its temperature 1°C. This quantity (100 calories/°C in this case) is called the object's *heat capacity*:

$$\textbf{heat capacity (in cal/°C)} = \frac{\textbf{heat absorbed (in cal)}}{\textbf{temperature change (in °C)}}$$

For example, a 100-g sample of water requires 100 calories to raise its temperature 1°C. Therefore, its heat capacity is 100 calories per degree Celsius. In the case of cooking oil, we found that 1,000 calories raised the temperature of 100 g by 20°C. Therefore, the heat capacity of 100 g of cooking oil is 1,000 calories divided by 20°C or 50 calories/°C, which is half that of water.

The heat capacity of an object indicates its ability to "store" or "soak up" heat. The greater an object's heat capacity, the more heat it can store at a given temperature. The larger an object's heat capacity, the more heat it must absorb for a given rise in temperature. Investigation 4.2 showed you that water stores about twice as much heat at a given temperature as an equal mass of cooking oil.

According to the fluid theory of heat it makes sense that heat capacity increases as the mass of an object increases. Just as a wide container holds more fluid than a narrow container at the same fluid level, a large object holds more heat than a small object at the same temperature.

A large body of water like a lake or ocean has a large heat capacity. That is why the temperature of these large bodies of water changes very slowly. The surface of the land around a lake or ocean, however, has a much smaller heat capacity. That is why the ground near a lake may be frozen while the lake water is still liquid.

Exploring on Your Own

- Place a bucket of cold water and a glassful of cold water in a warm room. Which sample of water reaches room temperature first? Why?

- Place an ice cube in a cup of cold water. At the same time, place an identical ice cube in an empty cup in a warm room. Which ice cube melts faster? Why?

Specific Heat

Dividing an object's heat capacity by its mass tells us how much heat is required to raise the temperature of just 1 g of the object's substance by 1°C. This quantity is called *specific heat*:

$$\textbf{specific heat (in cal/°C/g)} = \frac{\textbf{heat capacity (in cal/°C)}}{\textbf{mass (in g)}}$$

For example, the specific heat of water is 1 calorie per degree Celsius per gram because it takes 1 calorie to raise the temperature of 1 g of water by 1°C. We found that it requires about 1,000 calories to change the temperature of 100 g of cooking oil by 20°C, so its heat capacity was determined to be:

$$\textbf{heat capacity} = \frac{\textbf{1,000 cal}}{\textbf{20°C}} = \textbf{50 cal/°C}$$

Since the mass of the oil was 100 g, its specific heat is given by:

$$\text{specific heat} = \frac{\textbf{heat capacity}}{\textbf{mass}} = \frac{50 \text{ cal/}°\text{C}}{100 \text{ g}} = 0.50 \text{ cal/}°\text{C/g}$$

The specific heat of a substance shows the amount of heat *per gram* that the substance can absorb for each 1 degree increase in temperature. The greater an object's specific heat, the more heat each gram of it must absorb to raise its temperature by one degree.

The specific heat of air is about one-fifth the specific heat of water. Consequently, it takes about 5 times as much heat to warm up the cold water in a swimming pool as it does to warm up the air in all the rooms in a mansion if the air and water have the same mass.

The Fluid Theory of Heat, Specific Heat, and Density

Can the fluid theory of heat explain why different substances have different specific heats? One explanation might be that the size or the number of empty spaces between the particles of different substances are not the same. If one substance has more or bigger spaces than

TABLE 8: DENSITIES OF SOME SUBSTANCES		
Substance	Density (g/cm^3)	Volume occupied by 1 g (cm^3/g)
Air	0.0012	833
Ice	0.92	1.09
Water	1.0	1.0
Aluminum	2.7	0.37
Copper	8.9	0.11
Lead	11.3	0.088

another, it can fit more heat per gram into these spaces. This would be like two sponges with different size pores. The sponge with the larger pores can hold more fluid. Perhaps the spaces between water particles are greater than those between the particles of cooking oil.

You may know that *density* is the amount of mass found in a given volume. The more dense a substance is, the more mass it has per unit of volume. The more dense a substance, the smaller the volume a given mass occupies. You know that it is a lot easier to carry a pail of air than a pail of water, which is much denser than air.

The densities of several substances and the volumes that 1 g of each occupies is shown in Table 8. As you have seen before, the density of water is simply 1 g/mL or 1 g/cm^3. A cubic centimeter (cm^3) is the same volume as a milliliter.

What would Joseph Black's fluid theory of heat predict about the specific heat of high-density substances such as lead and copper compared to the specific heat of low-density substances such as water? According to the theory, a high-density substance has very little space between its particles. A substance of higher density should have a lower specific heat because it has less space to store that heat.

The fluid theory of heat would predict that lead should have a small specific heat. It would also predict that aluminum should have a specific heat greater than lead but less than water.

In the following investigation you will compare the specific heats of aluminum, copper, and lead. In doing so, you will be able to test one prediction made by the fluid theory of heat.

4.4 Comparing Specific Heats*

Use the balance to weigh out 100-g samples of aluminum, copper, and lead. Place the metals in a freezer. Leave them there for about an hour to be sure they reach the same low temperature as the freezer.

Pour 50 mL (50 g) of water at room temperature into one of the insulated cups. Measure the temperature of the water and record it in your notebook. Using tongs or a pot holder so that your hand will not heat the metal, remove the aluminum from the freezer and quickly put it into the water in the insulated cup. Swirl the water about the aluminum and record the final temperature of the metal-water mixture. What was the change in temperature of the water?

Things you'll need:

- balance
- about 100 g of aluminum pellets, nails, or tightly folded foil
- about 100 g of copper pennies, copper shot, or pieces of copper tubing
- about 100 g of lead (fishing sinkers, washers, or sheet metal)
- freezer
- tap water
- 2 insulated cups
- graduated cylinder
- laboratory thermometer
- tongs or pot holders
- ice

Repeat the experiment using the samples of copper and lead. Which metal lowers the water's temperature the most? Which cold metal, therefore, absorbed the most heat from the water? Which metal absorbed the least heat from the water? Which metal has the largest specific heat? Which metal has the smallest specific heat? Do your results agree with predictions made from the fluid theory of heat?

Now add 100 mL (100 g) of ice water (water at about 0°C) to a 50 mL (50 g) sample of water at room temperature. What is the final temperature of the mixture? How does the heat absorbed by the cold water compare with the heat absorbed by the even colder metals? How does the specific heat of water compare with the specific heat of these metals?

Exploring on Your Own

- Which has the greater heat capacity—a stack of two nickels or a stack of four nickels? To find out, place the two stacks side by side on a flat piece of ice. Watch the coins carefully. How can you tell which stack of coins has the larger heat capacity?

- Which coins have the greatest specific heat—pennies, nickels, dimes, or quarters? One way to find out is to place equal weights of these coins on a flat slab of ice. Which type of coin melts more ice? Measure the volume of the hole made by each stack of coins after they stop sinking into the ice by pressing clay into the hole. What do your results tell you? Which type of coin has the largest specific heat?

- Place 50 g each of water, copper (old pennies), lead (fishing sinkers), iron (nails), and aluminum (pellets, nails, or foil) in separate insulated cups. Leave them undisturbed for a few minutes so that all of them will be at room temperature. Fill a large bucket with hot tap water. Then add 50 mL (50 g) of the hot water to one of the cups. Stir and record the final temperature before doing the same thing to the next cup. Work as rapidly as possible so that the water temperature in the bucket does not change. Which of the materials in the cups has the largest specific heat? Which has the smallest?

- To actually measure the specific heat of aluminum, follow these steps:

    (1) Weigh out about 100 g of aluminum pellets, nails, or tightly rolled balls of aluminum foil. Record the exact mass in your notebook in a table like Table 9 (Do not write in this book.)

    (2) Place the aluminum in a dry insulated cup and put the cup

in a refrigerator for a few minutes to lower the temperature of the metal.

(3) After the aluminum has cooled for a few minutes, measure its temperature in the refrigerator.

(4) Pour 100 mL (100 g) of hot tap water into a second insulated cup and measure its temperature. Record both temperatures in your notebook in a table like Table 9.

(5) *Immediately after* measuring the temperature of the hot water, remove the aluminum from the refrigerator. Then pour the hot water into the insulated cup containing the aluminum. Stir and record the final temperature of the mixture.

TABLE 9: FINDING THE SPECIFIC HEAT OF ALUMINUM

	Aluminum	Water
Mass (grams)	100	100
Initial temperature (°C)		
Final temperature (°C)		
Temperature change (°C)		
Heat gained or lost (cal)		
Heat capacity (cal/°C)		
Specific heat (cal/°C/g)		1

When the water and the aluminum are mixed, heat passes from the hot water to the aluminum until their temperatures become equal. As you know, if this is done quickly the heat absorbed by the aluminum will equal the heat lost by the water.

Calculate the heat lost by the water using the equation:

Heat (cal) = **mass of water** (g) x **temperature change** (°C)

Enter this value in the table as both the heat gained by the aluminum and the heat lost by the water.

Calculate the heat capacity of the aluminum by dividing the heat gained by its temperature change. Then calculate the specific heat of the aluminum by dividing its heat capacity by its mass.

The specific heat of aluminum found from many carefully performed experiments is 0.22 calories/°C/g. How does your value compare with this one?

- Repeat the experiment to find the heat capacities of 100-gram samples of copper and lead. Then calculate their specific heats. How do the specific heats you measured compare to the values of 0.092 for copper and 0.031 for lead, values found from many carefully performed experiments?

The fluid theory of heat developed by Joseph Black has given us a way to measure heat as well as to explain it. The theory can explain why some substances, such as water, require more heat to raise their temperature than do other substances, such as cooking oil. It can also explain why dense substances have smaller specific heats than less dense ones, and why heat capacity increases with mass.

It is water's high specific heat and the large heat capacity of oceans and large lakes that moderates temperatures around the world. Summer temperatures near the ocean or near large lakes are generally cooler than temperatures far from these large bodies of water. The reason is that heat flows from warm air to the cooler water in these lakes and oceans. On the other hand, desert temperatures soar because the heat capacities of their soils are far less than lake and ocean waters. At night, desert temperatures may fall to the freezing point because the soil there holds so little heat, while temperatures near lakes and oceans remain moderate because heat now flows from the warmer water to the cooler air.

Sometimes when you add heat to something, there is no change in temperature. You've seen this when you've watched ice melt or water boil.

5

Melting, Boiling, and Hidden Heat

In addition to changing the temperature of a substance, heat can also change the physical states of matter. For example, when heat is added to ice, the ice melts. That is, heat can change water from a solid to a liquid. If enough heat is added to water, it will boil and change from a liquid to a gas.

Most substances can exist in a solid, a liquid, or a gaseous state. To make any substance melt or boil, heat must be added. To make a substance freeze or *condense* (change from a gas to a liquid), heat must be removed. The temperatures at which substances change state can be both very high and very low. Tungsten, the metal used to make light bulb filaments, is still a solid at 3,400°C (6,152°F). On the other hand, air is still a gas at -180°C (-292°F), and helium is still a gas at -265°C (-445°F).

In this chapter, you will investigate melting and boiling and their reverse processes, freezing and condensation. You can begin by measuring the temperature of melting ice.

5.1 Temperature and Melting Ice*

Place some of the crushed ice or snow into the small cup. Stir the ice or snow with the thermometer until the temperature stops changing. What is the temperature of the ice or snow? Is the ice or snow melting?

Using the same thermometer, measure the temperature of the

Things you'll need:

- gallon or more of crushed ice or snow
- thermometer
- small cup (medicine cup or paper cup)
- large container (bucket or gallon container)

melting ice or snow that fills the bucket. Does the amount of ice or snow affect the temperature at which it melts?

Exploring on Your Own

- Put a thermometer in a small container of water. Be sure the water completely covers the bulb of the thermometer, which should be held in place near the center of the water. Place this setup in a freezer and leave it there until the water is completely frozen. Remove the container from the freezer and put it in a protected place in a warm room. Measure the temperature of the ice at 5- or 10-minute intervals until it melts and reaches room temperature. Record your measurements in your notebook.

In your notebook, plot a graph of temperature versus time on axes like those shown in Figure 5-1. Draw a curved line by connecting all the points you have plotted. What does your graph look like? How does it compare with the authors' graph in Figure 5-1? How do you explain the level parts of the graph—that is, the parts where the line is parallel to the time axis?

Melting Ice and Hidden Heat

When you measured the temperature of melting ice in investigation 5.1, you found that the temperature remained constant. It did not increase as the ice melted, no matter how much ice was present. Yet heat must have been flowing into the ice; otherwise, none of it would have melted. This is what we mean by hidden heat; heat flows into the ice but its temperature does not change. This is unlike liquid water—its temperature rises when heat is added. In the next investigation, you will melt ice at a faster rate by using a flame. Let us see if the heat still remains hidden as the ice melts.

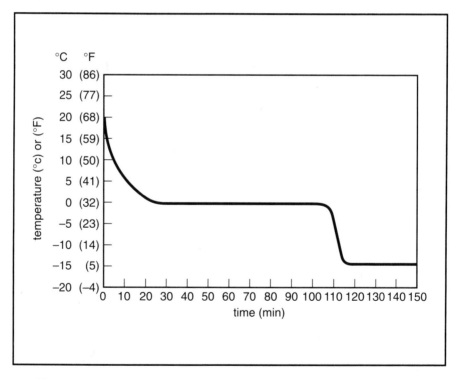

Figure 5-1) This graph of the authors' experimental results shows what happened when water at 20°C was placed in a freezer. How can you explain the two level parts of the graph where the line is parallel to the time axis?

5.2 Melting Ice Faster*

In this experiment you will use the candle just as you did in investigation 4.1 to see how the temperature of a mixture of ice and water changes as heat is added at a constant rate.

Things you'll need:

- same as investigation 4.1
- crushed ice or snow

(1) Fill the 6-oz frozen juice can about one-third full with the crushed ice or snow and press it down firmly. Pour in cold water until it just reaches the top surface of the ice. After mixing you should have a thick "slush."

(2) **With an adult present**, light the candle and heat the mixture with the candle flame. Raise the candle every few minutes to keep the flame just touching the can. This can be done by carefully squeezing the clay holder. Measure the temperature every 30 seconds until the mixture reaches room temperature. Stir the mixture slowly but constantly while it is heating. Record the temperatures and times in your notebook in a table like Table 10. (Do not write in this book.) To fill in the column under *heat*, you can assume that the candle produces heat at the same rate that it did in investigation 4–1.

(3) Use the results in your table to draw a temperature-versus-time, graph. What did you notice about the temperature as the ice melted? How much time passed before the water temperature started rising? How much heat was absorbed by the mixture before the temperature started to rise? What happened to most of the ice or snow before the temperature started to rise?

Exploring on Your Own

- Prepare two ice "cubes" that have equal volumes but different shapes. Make one in a regular cylindrical plastic container and the other in a wide flat plastic tray or dish cover so it has a pancake shape. When they are frozen, remove the two pieces of ice from

TABLE 10: TEMPERATURE AND HEAT VERSUS TIME FOR MELTING ICE		
Time (min)	Heat (cal)	Temperature (°C)
0.0	0	0
0.5		
1.0		
1.5		
2.0		
2.5		
3.0		
3.5		
4.0		
4.5		
5.0		
. . .		

their molds and place them in a bucket of water. Which piece of ice melts faster? How does the surface area of ice affect its melting time?

- Invent ways to make ice cubes that have different shapes but equal volumes. For example, make ice "cubes" that are spheres, cones, pyramids, cylinders, and so forth. Which shape melts fastest? Which one melts slowest? How is the melting rate of these different shapes related to their surface areas? How can you find their surface areas?

Just for Fun

- Make some funny-shaped ice "cubes." You can use cookie cutters, balloons, hollow toys, rubber gloves, and other containers to mold the ice. You might add food coloring to the water before you freeze it.

The Hidden Heat of Melting

You probably found in projects 5.1 and 5.2 that the temperature of melting ice or snow stayed near 0°C even though heat was flowing into the ice from the warm air or candle flame at a steady rate. You probably also observed that the temperature did not start to rise until most of the ice was melted.

Heat added to melting ice goes into melting the ice without changing its temperature. Therefore, according to Black's theory, liquid water at 0°C must have more heat stored in it than ice at 0°C. This stored heat is sometimes called *hidden heat* because it does not cause a temperature change. The hidden heat used to melt one gram of ice is called the *latent heat of melting*. In the next investigation you will find out how much heat is needed to melt a gram of ice.

5.3 The Latent Heat of Melting*

To measure the latent heat of melting, carry out the following steps.

(1) Use the graduated cylinder or measuring cup to measure out 50 mL (1.75 fluid oz) of tap water at room temperature. Pour the water into one of the insulated cups and measure its temperature with the thermometer.

(2) Dry off two of the ice cubes

Things you'll need:
- graduated cylinder or measuring cup
- tap water
- insulated cups
- thermometer
- ice cubes
- paper towels

with a paper towel and place the cubes in another insulated cup. Then pour the tap water over the ice cubes. Stir the mixture vigorously with the thermometer until the temperature reaches 0°C (32°F) or stops decreasing.

(3) Immediately pour the water back into the graduated cylinder, leaving the remaining ice in the cup. You will find that there is more water in the graduated cylinder now than when you started. Where did this extra water come from?

(4) Calculate the mass of ice that melted by subtracting the starting mass of tap water (50 g) from the final mass of the water. (Remember that the mass of 1 mL of water is 1 g).

When the tap water cooled from room temperature to 0°C, it lost heat. This heat was used to melt the ice also at 0°C. Therefore, the hidden heat used to melt the ice must equal the heat lost by the 50 g of tap water.

To calculate this hidden heat, use the equation:

Hidden heat = 50 g x temperature change of tap water

If the temperature of the 50 g of water fell from 20°C to 0°C, then the hidden heat used to melt the ice was 1,000 cal (50 g x 20°C).

To calculate the latent heat of melting, divide the hidden heat you have calculated by the mass of ice that melted. This will give you the heat needed to melt 1 g of ice. The ice that melted is, of course, the difference between the final mass of water and melted ice and the initial 50 g of water. For example, if the final mass of water was 65 g (65 mL) when the water temperature reaches 0°C, then the ice that melted is 15 g (65 g - 50 g = 15 g). If the hidden heat was 1,000 calories, the heat needed to melt 1 g of ice was 67 cal (1,000 calories/15 g), according to the results.

Many similar carefully performed experiments have shown that the latent heat of melting for water is 79 calories/g. How does your value compare?

Exploring on Your Own

- To determine how much heat is required to melt ice, Joseph Black compared the time it took for a certain mass of ice to melt and warm up to 5°C with the time it took for an equal amount of ice water to warm up from 0°C to 5°C. He placed the ice and the water in the same room and assumed that heat flowed into both at the same rate.

Just for Fun

You can do a similar experiment. Add one or two large ice cubes to a cup that you have already weighed. Quickly weigh the ice and cup together. Then set the cup aside and record the time. When the ice has completely melted, note the time again and determine how long it took for the ice to melt. How can you determine the mass of the ice from the data you have?

While the ice is melting in the first cup, add several ice cubes to a second cup half filled with water. Stir the mixture with your thermometer until the temperature of the water is 0°C. Then pour cold water from this cup into a third cup that is resting on a balance scale. Continue to pour until the weight of ice water in the cup is equal to the weight of the ice that you set aside to melt. (Do not forget that the cup has mass too.)

Record the time when you poured the ice water into the cup on the balance. When the water reaches 5°C, record the time again. How long did it take for the water temperature to rise from 0°C to 5°C?

Suppose that the time that it takes for the ice water to warm from 0° to 5° represents one unit of heat. How many units of heat were needed to melt the same mass of ice? How many times as much heat was needed to melt the ice as to warm the ice water from 0°C to 5°C?

Since you know the mass of the water in grams, you can multiply it by 5°C to find how many calories of heat were required to warm the water. How much heat, in calories, was needed to warm the cold water through 5°C? How much heat, in calories, was needed to melt the ice? How much heat, in calories, is needed to melt one gram of ice?

A list of latent heats of melting for different substances is shown in Table 11. In each case, the latent heat of melting is the heat needed to melt one gram of the substance.

TABLE 11: SOME LATENT HEATS OF MELTING	
Substance	Latent heat of melting (cal/g)
Water	79
Alcohol	25
Lead	5.9
Copper	42

Hidden Heat in Steam

When heat is added to liquid water, its temperature rises steadily until it starts to boil at 100°C. As the water boils, its temperature remains constant at 100°C. It is only after all the water has turned to steam that additional heat raises the *temperature* of the steam above 100°C.

This behavior is similar to that of melting. In both cases the heat changes the state (solid or liquid) of water without increasing its temperature. Therefore, steam at 100°C has more heat stored in it than liquid water at the same 100°C. This extra heat is the *hidden heat of vaporization*. The amount of heat needed to turn 1 g of water at 100°C into steam at the same temperature is called the *latent heat of vaporization*. In the next investigation you will measure the latent heat of vaporization of water using a method similar to the one used by Joseph Black.

5.4 The Latent Heat of Vaporization of Water*

Use the graduated cylinder or measuring cup to measure out 100 mL (about 3.5 oz) of tap water. Pour the water into the sauce pan and use the thermometer to measure its temperature. (If you are using a household thermometer, be sure to remove the thermometer before you heat the water.) **With an adult present,** turn on a stove burner and adjust to a medium flame. If you have an electric range or hot plate, turn the heating element to its highest setting and give it several minutes to heat up.

Things you'll need:
- graduated cylinder or measuring cup
- tap water
- small sauce pan
- thermometer
- safety goggles, gloves, long-sleeved shirt
- kitchen stove or hot plate

To avoid being burned by any water that might spatter, put on safety goggles and wear gloves and long sleeves. Then place the sauce pan on the stove or hot plate. Record the exact time that you begin heating the water. Record the time again when the water begins to boil. How long did it take to raise the temperature of the water to the boiling point (100°C)?

Finally, record the time when the last bit of water has boiled away. **Then quickly remove the pan and turn off the stove. The pan itself might be damaged if not removed from the heat right away.**

How long did it take to boil away all the water after it reached the boiling point? How does the time required to boil away all the water compare with the time it took to raise the water from its initial temperature to the boiling point? Assume, as Black did, that heat flows into the water at a steady rate. How many times as much heat was required to boil all the water away as was needed to bring the water from its initial temperature to the boiling point?

Since it takes 1 cal of heat to raise the temperature of 1 g of water

1°C, how much heat was needed to raise the temperature of the water from its initial temperature to the boiling point? How can you use this value to find the heat needed to boil away all the water once it reached the boiling point? Use this calculation and the data you have to find the latent heat of vaporization for water. What is the value you calculate?

Exploring on Your Own

- To find the latent heat of vaporization more accurately, carry out the following experiment.

(1) **With an adult present,** turn on a stove burner to a medium flame. If you have an electric range or hot plate, turn the heating element to its highest setting and give it several minutes to heat up.

(2) Pour 500 mL or 18 oz (500 g) of cold tap water into a sauce pan and measure its temperature.

(3) Place the pan on the burner for 1 minute. **Be sure to wear safety goggles and long sleeves to avoid being burned by any water that might spatter**. Then remove the pan from the stove and measure the final water temperature.

(4) Calculate the amount of heat the stove delivers to the water in one minute by multiplying the change in temperature of the water, in degrees Celsius, by 500 g.

(5) Rinse the pan with cool water, dry it off, and then refill it with 100 mL (100 g) of cool water.

(6) Place the pan on the stove and measure the time it takes the 100 mL (100 g) of water to completely boil away.

(7) Calculate the total heat added to the water by multiplying the number of minutes it took the water to boil away by the amount of heat the stove delivered to the water every minute.

Of the total heat added to the water, some of it went into raising the water's temperature from its starting point to 100°C. This part of the total heat can be calculated using the equation:

heat to warm water to 100°C = 100 g × (100°C - initial temperature)

The rest of the heat, which changed the water into steam, is the hidden heat of vaporization.

(8) To calculate the hidden heat of vaporization, use the equation:

hidden heat of vaporization = total heat - heat to raise water temp. to 100°C

(9) Finally, calculate the latent heat of vaporization by dividing the hidden heat of vaporization by 100 g.

The heat of vaporization of water as determined by many carefully performed experiments is 540 calories/g. How does this compare with your value? How does the latent heat of vaporization compare with the latent heat of melting? What does this tell you about the amount of heat stored in steam? The latent heats of vaporization for several substances are shown in Table 12.

TABLE 12: SOME LATENT HEATS OF VAPORIZATION	
Substance	Latent heat of vaporization (cal/g)
Water	540
Hydrogen	110
Lead	206
Copper	1,160

Exploring on Your Own

- Leave some water in a saucer near an open window. What happens to the amount of water in the saucer after several hours? After several days? Does water change from a liquid to a gas at temperatures below 100°C?

- When water evaporates, it changes from a liquid to a gas. Does it absorb heat when it changes? To find out, place equal amounts of water at room temperature in three aluminum pie pans. Submerge a thermometer in each pan. Cover one pan with plastic wrap so water cannot escape. Leave a second pan uncovered, but in a place where air is not moving. Put a third pan, without a cover, in a breezy place or in front of a fan. **If you use a fan, ask an adult to watch you use it**. In which pan or pans does the temperature change? How does it change? How can you explain any temperature changes you observe? Are the results of this experiment different on a humid day than on a dry day?

Just for Fun

One simple way to see that heat is absorbed when water evaporates is to spread a little water on the back of your hand. Then wave your hand through the air. Notice how much cooler your hand feels. The hidden heat needed to change the water from a liquid to a gas comes from your body. As heat flows from your body to the water, it makes your skin feel colder.

You might also try the same experiment with rubbing alcohol which evaporates more rapidly than water.

Cooling Curves

If you performed the experiment immediately following project 5.1, you know what a warming curve for ice looks like. You found that the temperature of the ice rises until it reaches the melting point (0°C). Then the temperature remains constant while the ice melts.

Temperature versus time graphs can show many important features of the melting and boiling processes. The temperature versus time graph shown in Figure 5-2 shows what happens when a small sample of water, which starts as steam at 140°C, is cooled by removing heat at a steady rate until it is solid ice at -20°C.

The downward-sloping portions of the graph occur when the water is all in one state, that is, when it is all a gas (steam), a liquid, or a solid

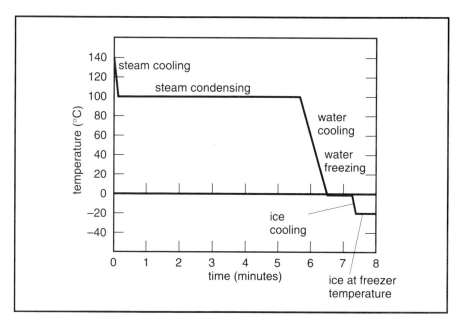

Figure 5-2) A temperature versus time graph for 1 g of water cooled from 140°C to -20°C.

(ice). During these times, the loss of heat causes the temperature to drop.

The level or horizontal sections of the graph—often called "plateaus"—indicate the temperatures at which water freezes or melts (0°C) and condenses or boils (100°C). These plateaus show us that while water is melting or freezing or boiling or condensing, its temperature stays constant even though heat is flowing out of the water.

The steepness of the graph is greater for cooling ice (from 0° to -20°) than it is for cooling liquid water (from 100° to 0°). It takes less heat to produce the same temperature change in ice than it does in liquid water. This tells us that ice has a smaller specific heat than water. The graph also shows that steam has a smaller specific heat than liquid water.

In practice, it is very difficult to remove heat at a steady rate. It is much easier to let an object simply stand in cooler surroundings and cool "naturally." Temperature-time graphs made when substances cool in this way are called cooling curves.

• An example of such a cooling curve is shown in Figure 5-3. The substance cooled was paradichlorobenzene (PDB), the chemical found in moth crystals. About 10 g of PDB was placed in a test tube and melted by placing it in hot water. The test tube was then allowed to cool "naturally" along with the water. For comparison, the temperature of the water in which the PDB was placed was recorded too. Its cooling curve is shown on the same graph.

There are several interesting features on this cooling curve. Each has been numbered on the graph (Figure 5-3).

(1) The graph gets less steep as it reaches the freezing plateau. This confirms the second rule of temperature change. As the temperature difference between the PDB and the surroundings get smaller, the rate of temperature change slows down.

(2) There is a slight dip in temperature just *before* freezing begins. This is because the PDB briefly remains a liquid even though its

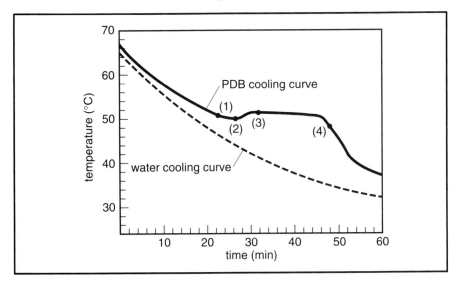

Figure 5-3) A cooling curve made when hot liquid PDB was allowed to cool in a beaker of water.

temperature is below its freezing temperature. This is called *super-cooling*. It is common in many substances, including water, which often undergoes supercooling in clouds before forming ice crystals that fall as sleet or snow.

(3) The freezing plateau at about 50°C is not perfectly flat but rises slightly for a time. This rise is caused by the release of hidden heat from the liquid as it freezes. During this time, more hidden heat is released from the PDB than is absorbed by the cooler surroundings. As a result, the temperature rises slightly above the freezing point.

(4) Immediately after the PDB completely freezes, the temperature drops very rapidly. This change happens because the temperature of the surrounding water continues to drop while the temperature of the PDB remains constant during its freezing. When the freezing is complete, the temperature difference between the PDB and the water is large, causing the PDB to cool rapidly, as we would predict from rule 2.

Exploring on Your Own

• Place 50 mL of hot water in one container. Place 150 mL of hot water at the same temperature in a second identical container. Measure their temperatures as they cool and plot both cooling curves on the same graph. See if you can predict which sample will cool faster. Were you right? When does each sample of water cool fastest? When does each sample of water cool slowest? How is this related to the rules of temperature change?

Substances with No Distinct Melting Temperature.

Not all substances have distinct melting points. For example, butter does not turn from a solid to a liquid at a precise temperature. Rather, it goes through a gradual softening process. Other examples of substances with no distinct melting points are tar and glass.

A cooling curve for corn oil margarine is shown in Figure 5-4. Does margarine have a sharp melting point?

Explaining Hidden Heat

You have learned how the fluid theory of heat explains the rules of temperature change, thermal expansion, and differences in the specific heats of substances. Can the fluid theory of heat also explain the hidden heat of melting and vaporization?

As you have seen, when heat is added to a solid, the solid expands. The fluid theory of heat says that heat particles fill the spaces between the solid's particles and push them apart. Melting might be the result of the heat finally pushing so hard on the particles that they break apart to form a free flowing liquid. When this happens, more space is suddenly created. The hidden heat of melting might be the heat needed

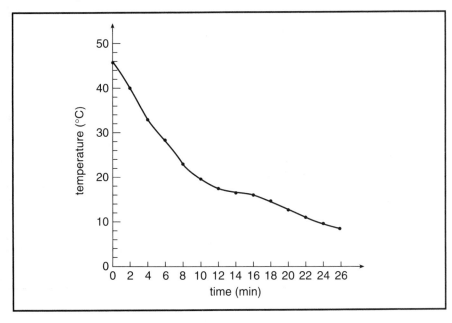

Figure 5-4) A cooling curve for corn oil margarine.

to fill this new space. Only after this newly created space is filled does additional heat start raising the liquid's temperature.

A similar explanation might be given for the hidden heat of vaporization. Heat expands a liquid and increases its temperature until it finally "blows it apart" into a vapor. Only after this newly created space is filled does additional heat start raising the vapor's temperature.

This explanation might sound good, but just because it makes sense does not mean that it is true. Every scientific explanation must be tested to see if it holds true under many different circumstances. One must always be open to other ideas that might explain more facts. You will see shortly that the fluid theory of heat has some serious drawbacks.

Hidden Heat and the Natural World

The fact that it takes nearly 80 calories of heat to melt a gram of ice means that ice and snow melt slowly, as you well know. If this were not true, we would find a very different world, one described by Joseph Black more than 200 years ago: "Were the ice and snow to melt suddenly . . . the torrents and inundations would be incomparably more irresistible and dreadful. They would tear up and sweep away everything."

If hidden heat were not required to change water from a liquid to a gas, the liquid would suddenly become a gas at 100°C. Since steam occupies about 1,700 times as much space as an equal mass of water, there would be a tremendous explosion every time a volume of water reached 100°C and changed to steam.

In Chapter 6 you will investigate how heat moves from place to place. From the furnace in the basement of your house or apartment to the air in your living room, from the sun to the earth, or from one end of a wire to another. You will also see that the fluid model of heat has difficulty explaining some of the ways in which heat moves.

6

The Motion of Heat

In previous investigations, you concluded that heat can move. In fact, the idea that heat flows like a fluid is a central part of the fluid theory of heat. According to the theory, the temperature of an object changes when heat flows into it or out of it. Substances melt, freeze, vaporize, or condense when hidden heat (heat that does not change their temperature) enters or leaves them.

In this chapter, you will investigate the motion of heat in more detail. By carefully comparing the motion of heat with the motion of real fluids, you may find more evidence that supports the fluid theory of heat. You may also find evidence that does *not* support the fluid theory of heat. Remember, we have no proof that heat is actually a fluid. After all, it cannot be seen, weighed, or separated from normal matter. All we know as fact are the rules of temperature change and the similarities between these rules and the rules of fluid level change. The rest is theory.

Heat Flow by Conduction

According to the fluid theory of heat, heat moves by *flowing* through substances in contact with each other just as a fluid flows between connected containers. This type of motion is called *thermal* conduction. Not all substances conduct heat with equal ease. Heat flows rapidly through some materials and quite slowly through others. The measure of a substance's ability to conduct heat is its *thermal conductivity*. The greater the thermal conductivity of a substance, the faster heat flows through it.

Substances with low thermal conductivities are called *insulators*. Substances with large thermal conductivities are called *conductors*. In the following investigation, you will compare the thermal conductivities of three different substances. You will also determine if the substances are best described as insulators or conductors.

6.1 Thermal Conductivities of Steel, Glass, and Insulation*

To compare the thermal conduction of steel, glass, and insulation, fill the large bucket or basin with a mixture of ice and cold tap water to a depth of about 2 in (5 cm). Next, fill the steel can with hot tap water and measure its initial temperature.

Put the can of hot water into the ice water and use the thermometer to measure its temperature every minute until it reaches 10°C. Record the temperatures and times in a table.

Repeat the experiment using the glass jar with the same amount of hot water at the same initial temperature. Perform the experiment a third time using the insulated cup.

Things you'll need:

- large bucket or basin of ice water
- ice
- hot and cold tap water
- 8-oz steel can
- thermometer
- watch or stopwatch
- 8-oz glass jar or beaker about as thick as the steel can
- 8-oz insulated cup (Styrofoam or other insulator)

On a temperature versus time graph plot the results of each experiment. How can you decide which substance is the best conductor of heat? Which is the worst conductor or the best insulator? Why are coffee cups *not* made of steel? Why are cooking pans often made of steel?

Exploring on Your Own

- Make some flat pieces of ice by freezing water in wide shallow plastic dishes or trays. Place different objects on the ice. You might use paper clips, pieces of wood, thumbtacks, an eraser, chalk, coins, and washers. Which objects sink into the ice quickly? Which do not sink quickly? Can you explain why some materials cause the ice under them to melt quickly and others do not?

Comparing Heat Conductors

In the next investigation you will see whether there are differences in the conductivities of different metals.

6.2 A Heat Conduction Race

Fill one of the small glass jars with chunks of canning wax. **With an adult present**, bring water to a boil in the sauce pan on the stove or hot plate. Then melt the wax by placing the jar in the pan of gently boiling water.

Put on the gloves. Coat the three lengths of wire with wax by dipping first one end and then the other into the melted wax. It is important to dip the wire in and out of the wax rapidly. Let the wax harden on the wire.

Make this setup in a large sink. Lay the coated wires across the top of another glass jar as shown in Figure 6-1. The ends should touch

Things you'll need:

- three small glass jars
- canning wax
- sauce pan
- tap water
- stove or hot plate
- gloves
- one 4-in (10 cm) length of 18 gauge copper wire
- one 4-in (10 cm) length of 18 gauge aluminum wire
- one 4-in (10 cm) length of 18 gauge steel wire
- modeling clay
- small candle
- large sink

each other at one end and spread apart at the other.

Form the clay into a candle holder and put the candle into it. Adjust the height of the candle so that the tip of the wick is just below the ends of the wires. Then light the candle away from the wires.

Continue to work in the sink, where there are no drafts to disturb a flame. After giving the candle flame a few seconds to even out, carefully slide the jar to place the touching wire ends in the center of the flame. Fill the third glass jar with tap water.

Observe how the wax melts along the lengths of the three wires. When the wax is almost completely melted off the "fastest" wire, pour a small amount of cold water from the third glass jar over all the wires and the candle. This will "freeze the action" at that moment.

Measure the distances that the wax melted along each wire. Which metal is the best conductor? Which is the worst?

Table 13 lists the thermal conductivities of different substances. The values represent the number of calories of heat that can pass through a 1-cm cube of the substance in 1 minute when the temperature difference between opposite sides is just 1°C. The substances are listed in order of their thermal conductivities with the best conductors at the top and the best insulators at the bottom. How did your results from investigation 6.2 compare with those in the table?

Note that air is one of the best insulators. This property of air is what makes Styrofoam and glass wool such good insulators. Both are filled with tiny pockets of trapped air that greatly slow the flow of heat. The same principle applies to the fiberglass insulation used in homes, and to the insulating fibers in winter clothing.

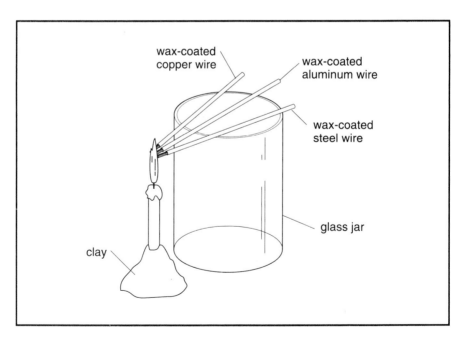

Figure 6-1) Comparing thermal conductivity.

TABLE 13. SOME THERMAL CONDUCTIVITIES	
Substance	Thermal conductivity (cal/cm/°C/min)
Silver	58.2
Copper	55.2
Aluminum	29.4
Steel	7.2
Glass	0.12
Wood	0.012
Air	0.0040
Styrofoam	0.0034

Exploring on Your Own

• Put 100 mL of hot tap water into each of five different containers—a tin can, a paper cup, a plastic cup, an insulated cup, and an insulated cup with an insulating cover. Place all five cups side by side and measure the temperature in each cup at 2-minute intervals. Plot a temperature-versus-time curve for each cup, all on the same graph.

   In which cup did the water cool fastest? In which cup did the water cool slowest? Which material is the best insulator? Does a cover affect the rate at which a liquid cools?

• Challenge some friends to an "ice-cube-keeping race." See who can keep an ice cube frozen for the longest time. Of course, you will want to establish some rules first, such as banning the use of freezers and refrigerators.

A Problem for the Fluid Theory of Heat

To explain conduction, Joseph Black's fluid theory of heat suggests that heat moves through the spaces between the particles of a substance. As a consequence of this theory, substances with low densities should have the highest thermal conductivities. This is because low-density substances have large spaces between their particles, making it easy for heat to move through them.

However, experiments show that low-density substances have the poorest thermal conductivity. Air is a perfect example. Dense metals, such as copper, conduct heat better than light metals such as aluminum.

This is an important flaw in the fluid theory of heat. However, it does not mean that you should immediately reject the fluid theory. One flaw does not eliminate all the good points of a theory. Like any good scientist, you would probably continue to use this theory, even though it is flawed, until someone devised a better one. Otherwise, you would be left with nothing to explain your observations or from which to make predictions about the results of new experiments.

Heat Conduction: Other Factors

Factors other than density affect the rate of heat conduction. One factor is temperature difference. In Chapter 3 you found that the greater the difference in temperature between two touching bodies, the faster their temperatures changed. The fluid theory of heat explained this fact by saying that large temperature differences mean large differences in heat levels between two objects. This difference leads to a rapid flow of heat fluid and, therefore, a rapid temperature change.

Another factor that affects the rate of heat flow is the amount of exposed surface an object has. For example, water will boil much faster in a wide, shallow pan than in a tall narrow pan. The wide pan has more surface area touching the hot stove, so it can absorb heat. Similarly, a large pipe can transport more water in a given amount of time than a narrow pipe.

The surface area factor in heat conduction has several important applications. One is seen in the design of car radiators that use air flow to cool the circulating coolant. If you look at such a radiator, you will see that it looks like a honeycomb. The many small openings increase the surface area exposed to the cool air. In houses, radiators designed to transfer heat to the surrounding air are made with many fins or coils that provide a large surface area for escaping heat. The same principle is used in the car radiators. On the other hand, pipes that bring steam or hot water from a furnace to the radiators are straight and usually covered with insulation so that as little heat as possible is lost between the furnace and the radiators.

A third factor affecting the rate of heat flow is the distance heat has to travel. In cold climates, thick blankets of fiberglass insulation are used in the walls and ceilings of buildings to reduce the rate of heat flow to the outside air.

Exploring on Your Own

- Place an ice cube on a paper towel. Break the cube into small pieces with a hammer. Leave an identical ice cube in one piece. Place both the whole and the crushed cube into separate but equal volumes of water in identical cups. Which ice will melt faster? Why do you think so? Were you right?

- Place an ice cube in a cup of cold water. Place an identical ice cube in a cup of hot water. Which ice cube will melt faster? Why do you think so?

- Prepare two cups. One should be a single insulated cup. The second should consist of several insulated cups stacked together to make a thicker wall. Place identical ice cubes in both containers and cover them with inverted insulated cups—a single cup on the first one; several stacked cups on the second one. In which container will the ice melt faster? Why do you think so? Were you right?

Convection

If you pick up an object and move it, the heat that is in the object moves with it. When you carry a cup of hot water across the room, the heat in the cup takes a ride too. In many homes, heat from the furnace is "carried" to the many different rooms by hot air or by water or steam that is pumped through pipes. This is much more efficient than moving the heat by conduction alone, that is, by leaving objects in contact with each other.

Almost everyone has heard the phrase "hot air rises." This is a rule of nature that makes hot air balloons possible. When the air in a balloon is heated, it expands and becomes less dense than the cooler air around it. The less dense air is forced upward like a bubble released from the bottom of a lake. The heat in the warm air is carried upward too.

It is not necessary for air to be inside a balloon to rise. Whenever any quantity of air is heated to a temperature greater than the surrounding air, it rises. This is true for all gases and liquids. The motion of heat brought about by the natural rising of a warmed fluid is called *convection*. In the next investigation, you will study the convection process in water.

6.3 Convection in Liquids*

To observe convection in a liquid, fill the cup with hot tap water. Add several drops of food coloring and stir. Then fill the large, clear jar or bowl with cold water. Next, remove the rubber bulb from the eye dropper and submerge the tube in the hot colored water. When the tube is full, place your thumb or finger

Things you'll need:

- clear cup or other container
- tap water
- dark food coloring
- large, clear jar or bowl
- eye dropper

firmly over the top end and remove it from the water. If you keep your finger tightly pressed on the tube, the colored water should not drain out (see Figure 6-2).

Now, keeping the dropper tube upright, submerge it all the way to the bottom of the jar of clear, cold water. Remove your finger from the tube. From which end does the hot colored water come out? Does

Figure 6-2) Removing water with a tube.

the motion of the colored water resemble smoke coming out a chimney?

Repeat this experiment with cold, colored water in the dropper and warm water in the large jar. What differences do you observe? Finally, repeat the experiment with the colored water at the same temperature as the surrounding water.

Convection is a very common and important process in nature. On a sunny day, when air over warm land near the ocean is heated, it rises. Cooler air from over the ocean moves in to replace it (Figure 6-3). The result is a wind that we commonly call an on-shore-breeze or sea breeze. Similarly, hot air heated by a fire in a fireplace carries smoke up a chimney rather than back into the house.

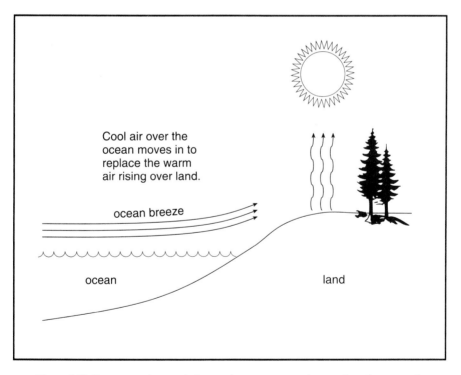

Figure 6-3) On a sunny day, cool air over the ocean moves in to replace the warm air rising over land.

Heat Motion by Radiation

The third and final way in which heat can travel is by *radiation*. The most obvious example of radiation is sunlight, which travels 94,000,000 miles (150,000,000 kilometers) through empty space and warms our planet. Since there is no air in most of the space between the earth and the sun, the heat cannot travel by conduction or convection. Other examples of radiation are the heat from fires and light bulb filaments. The microwaves that warm food and the X-rays used to make images of our skeletons are also forms of radiation. Infrared radiation is one way that heat is emitted from buildings and your own body.

It is easy to prove that heat transfer by radiation is completely different from conduction and convection. If you hold your hand up to the Sun, the side facing it immediately feels warmer than the surrounding air. Solar radiation is warming your hand directly without warming the surrounding air. If this warming had occurred by conduction, your hand would only get as hot as the surrounding air. If convection were responsible, you would feel a warm breeze blowing toward your hand.

In the following investigation, you will study some of the properties of radiation. You will also discover how the amount of radiant heat absorbed by an object depends on its color.

6.4 Radiation, Heating, and Color*

To investigate how heating by radiation depends on color, use the scissors to cut four strips of the aluminum foil 12 in (30 cm) long and 1.5 in (3 cm) wide (Figure 6-4a). Make each aluminum strip into a tube by rolling it tightly around the thermometer. Secure the free end with a very small piece of the tape and remove the thermometer. Use the paint brush and paints to paint one tube black, another white, and another blue. Leave the fourth tube unpainted.

Things you'll need:

- scissors
- aluminum foil
- ruler
- laboratory thermometer
- tape
- small paint brush
- black, white, and blue paint
- desk lamp with a 60-, 75- or 100-watt light bulb
- clock or watch

Adjust the desk lamp so that the light bulb is about 4 in (10 cm) from the table top (see Figure 6-4b). Insert the thermometer bulb into the unpainted foil tube and rest it directly under the light bulb. Record the starting temperature in a table in your notebook. Then turn on the light. Measure and record the temperature once every minute for 5 minutes. Repeat the experiment with each of the painted tubes.

Which tube reached the highest temperature? Which color absorbed the most radiation? Which absorbed the least? On the basis of what you observed, can you explain why houses in warm climates are often painted white and why people wear light colored clothing in the summer months? Why do you feel warmer when you wear dark summer clothes?

Exploring on Your Own

- Hold your hand below a light bulb and turn on the light. Can you feel heat coming from the bulb immediately? Could the heat have reached your hand by convection? Could the heat have reached your hand by conduction?

• Turn on a light and place a large glass jar upside down over the bulb. While the jar is still cool, hold your hand *near* the *side* of the jar. Can you feel the heat coming from the bulb? Is your hand warmer than the jar? Could the heat have reached your hand by conduction? Could the heat have reached your hand by convection? How is the heat getting to your hand?

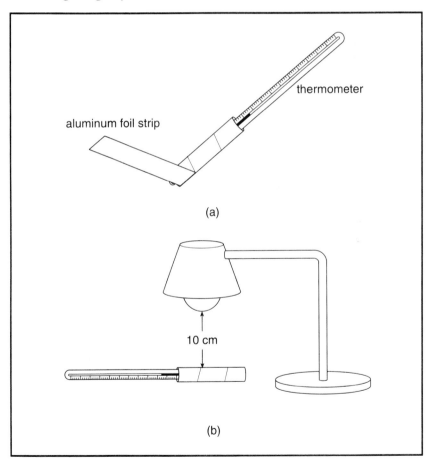

(a)

(b)

Figure 6-4) Testing for radiant heat flow.

- Obtain two identical, shiny, tin cans. Paint one can black and let it dry. Then pour the same amount of cold water into both cans. Record the water temperature in both cans and place them in bright sunlight or beside a bright lamp. In which can does the water temperature increase faster? Can you explain why?

Just for Fun

- Find as many ways possible to make an ice cube melt faster than it melts in air.

A Strange Property of Radiation

You have learned that air is not a good conductor of heat. Yet, plenty of the Sun's heat reaches the Earth by radiation even though it must pass through the Earth's thick atmosphere. Similarly, standing behind a glass window hardly seems to stop the Sun's heat from warming you even though glass, like air, is a good insulator. How can substances stop heat when it moves by conduction but let heat through when it moves by radiation? It seems difficult to imagine that a real fluid could behave in this way.

This mysterious property of radiation poses another serious problem for the fluid theory of heat. When added to the other flaws in this theory (weightlessness, invisibility, and the greater conductivity of denser substances), one cannot help wondering if there might not be a better way to explain the rules of temperature change and other temperature related processes. In Chapter 7 you will investigate some of the other difficulties associated with the fluid theory of heat. Then you will try to develop another way of explaining the rules of temperature.

7

Another Theory of Heat

People have known since pre-historic times that objects can be made warmer if they are rubbed together. Just rub your hands together and see how warm they become. Early on, humans discovered that rubbing two sticks together can make them hot enough to burn.

Why does rubbing make hands, sticks, and other things warmer? According to the fluid theory of heat, an object becomes warmer when heat flows into it from a warmer object. But where does the heat come from when objects are warmed by rubbing? It cannot come from the surrounding air by conduction, because sometimes the air is colder than the object rubbed. Can the warming be explained by convection or radiation?

In the following investigation you will see if a substance can be warmed by shaking it inside a well-insulated container that is shielded from any radiation.

7.1 Creating Heat by Shaking

Use the scissors to cut out a cardboard circle that fits snugly into the bottom of one of the insulated cups (Figure 7-1). Tape the cardboard securely in place. Then pour all the pennies into the cup. After several minutes, measure the temperature of the pennies by gently inserting the thermometer under them.

Cut out another cardboard circle slightly larger than the opening of the cup. Tape it securely over the top of the cup.

Things you'll need:

- scissors
- cardboard (corrugated cardboard from a carton is best)
- insulated cups
- cellophane tape
- 50 pennies
- laboratory thermometer
- watch or clock

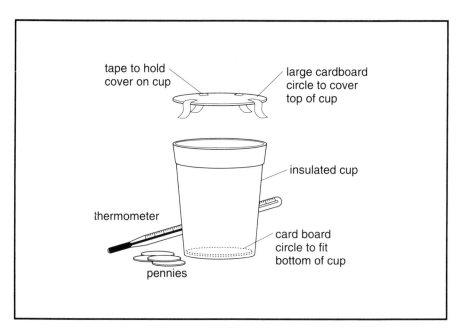

tape to hold cover on cup

large cardboard circle to cover top of cup

insulated cup

thermometer

card board circle to fit bottom of cup

pennies

Figure 7-1) Creating heat by shaking.

Now, shake the pennies in the cup vigorously for 4 minutes. Be sure you support both the top and bottom of the cup to prevent the pennies from breaking through. After 4 minutes, remove the top, insert the thermometer beneath the pennies and measure their temperature again. Take the reading after the temperature stops rising.

Did shaking cause the temperature of the pennies to change? Could this have come from thermal radiation? To see if the temperature change came from heat conducted to the cup by your warm hands, repeat the experiment without shaking and just hold the cup in your hands for 4 minutes. How much does the temperature change when you do this? Was the heat conducted from your hands enough to account for the temperature change of the pennies when you shook them?

Another Problem for the Fluid Theory of Heat

Investigation 7.1 shows that heat can be produced by shaking. This cannot be explained by the fluid theory of heat, because it seems as if heat is being created inside the pennies from nothing. But this goes against the idea that heat is conserved.

The fluid theory of heat was successful in explaining the rules of temperature change and other temperature effects. However, you have seen that this theory is seriously flawed. First, heat, unlike other fluids, seems to be completely weightless and invisible. Second, heat is easily conducted through dense metals even though there should be less space between particles for the heat to travel through. At the same time, heat is not conducted well by low–density gases even though they have plenty of space between particles. Third, heat is able to pass easily through glass when it travels by radiation but not when it travels by conduction. Finally, heat seems to be created from nothing by rubbing or shaking.

Heat, Motion, and the Kinetic Theory

Rubbing or shaking objects involves stopping or slowing their motion by friction. Friction seems to be the key to raising temperature by rubbing. For example, if you simply wave your hand, its temperature does not change. Only when there is friction between your hand and another object, such as your other hand, does it warm up. Shaking a single stick through the air will not start a fire because there is very little friction between the stick and the air.

The idea that heat is produced when an object's speed decreases was the starting point of an entirely new theory of heat and temperature change. This theory, known as the *kinetic theory*, maintains that heat is *not* a fluid. According to the kinetic theory, temperature is simply a side effect of the motions of the atoms and molecules of which all things are made. While an object as a whole may be at rest, its atoms or molecules, according to the kinetic theory, are continuously moving. In solids, these motions are the to-and-fro vibrations of atomic and molecular particles, which cannot be seen but can be felt. Rapid vibrations are felt as high temperatures; gentle vibrations are felt as low temperatures. In other words, temperature is simply a measure of the average speed of these particles.

According to the kinetic theory, when the motion of a solid object is stopped or slowed by friction, the motion does not simply disappear. Instead, it is converted into the invisible vibrations of its atoms. In this way the motion is conserved. It changes from the overall motion of the object into the rapid but tiny motions of its atoms.

An early proponent of the kinetic theory was Benjamin Thompson. Born in Massachusetts in 1753, Thompson served as a British spy before fleeing to England at the start of the American Revolution. After serving as a British officer during the war, he moved to Bavaria. While in Bavaria, Thompson distinguished himself as scientist, engineer, and inventor. He studied the insulating properties of clothing, discovered convection, and invented such practical items as the kitchen range, the double boiler, and the baking oven.

Thompson is most famous for two series of experiments that challenged the fluid theory of heat. In the first, he used the most precise scales of his time to carefully weigh objects as they cooled. The fact that they lost no weight convinced him that heat was not a real substance. Thompson's second series of experiments took place while he was in charge of the military arsenal in Munich, Germany. Using a cannon-boring machine to grind a blunt iron borer against a hollowed iron cylinder, he produced enough heat to boil large amounts of water surrounding the machine (See Figure 7-2). Since the entire device was well insulated, large quantities of heat were apparently being continually created from nothing. Thompson knew that the fluid theory could not explain how this heat was being created. The results, he argued, were better explained by the kinetic theory.

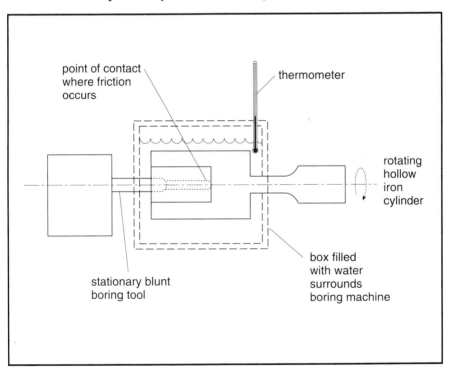

Figure 7-2) Benjamin Thompson's machine for producing heat by friction.

A Model of Matter

The kinetic theory is based on the idea that matter is made up of very small particles called atoms. This idea was first proposed by the Greek philosopher Democritus nearly 2,400 years ago. But not until the late 1700s did scientists begin to realize that the idea of atoms could explain many of the processes observed in nature.

Individual atoms and molecules were and still are far too small to be seen directly, even with the most powerful optical microscope. For this reason, scientists had no way of knowing whether atoms were real. Like heat fluid, atoms were part of a theory.

Although scientists could not see atoms directly, they could form mental images or *models* of them. At first, atoms were thought to be indestructible spheres. Each pure substance consisted of a large number

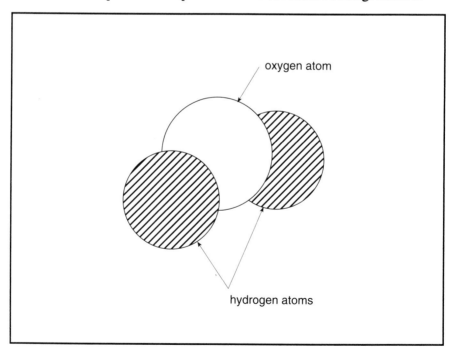

Figure 7-3) A model of a water molecule.

of identical atoms bonded together. Later, when some pure substances were separated into even simpler ones, scientists imagined that different atoms could bond to each other in specific ways to form molecules. Substances made from only one type of atom were called *elements*. Substances made by combining different atoms into molecules were called *compounds*. An example of a compound is water. Its molecule is made from two atoms of hydrogen and one atom of oxygen (See Figure 7-3).

You have learned that matter can exist as a solid, a liquid, or a gas, depending on the temperature. These three states of matter may be explained in terms of the different ways that atoms or molecules are joined together or bonded. In the following investigation, you will build a simple model of matter to show this relationship. You will also learn that this model can be used to explain the processes of melting, vaporization, thermal expansion, and conduction, as well as the rules of temperature change. In other words, this model can explain all the processes that the fluid theory explained. It also explains the nature of matter itself. The kinetic theory of heat explains more facts than the fluid theory. Therefore, it is a much broader, more inclusive theory.

7.2 A Model of Matter*

Place the marbles in the tray. Then tip the tray at an angle so that the marbles all collect at one end, as shown in Figure 7-4. Notice how they line up in a definite pattern of straight rows. This arrangement of marbles represents the arrange-

Things you'll need:

- 50 or more marbles (enough to cover about one-fourth of the tray)
- small tray with steep sides or a small shallow box

ment of atoms (or molecules) in *solid* matter. You might imagine that the atoms are held together in their tightly packed and ordered arrangement by attractive forces called chemical bonds.

Keeping the tray tilted at the same angle, jiggle it gently but rapidly in your hands. Notice how the marbles vibrate while staying in the same ordered arrangement. This represents a solid at some given temperature. The jiggling marbles represent vibrating atoms or molecules. The larger their vibrations the higher the temperature.

Now, decrease the tilt of the tray and gradually increase the amount of jiggling. Notice how the marbles no longer stay in their ordered rows. Even though they are still grouped together, they now constantly change positions, move over greater distances, and leave small open spaces between each other. Also, as you turn the tray, the marbles "flow" as a group. This condition of the model represents a *liquid.*

In a liquid the atoms are not as ordered or as tightly packed as in a solid. This is because at higher temperatures the larger vibrations allow the atoms to *momentarily* break away from their neighbors and to form bonds with new atoms. This results in a loss of order, more open spaces, and the ability of the atoms to flow. This is what happens when a substance *melts.*

Now place the tray on a *flat* surface and shake it vigorously. Notice how the marbles fill the entire tray, bouncing off each other and the walls in a chaotic manner. The marbles no longer jiggle but "fly" in straight lines until they collide with other marbles or the walls of the tray. This condition of the model represents a *gas*.

At high enough temperatures, which correspond to vigorous shaking in our model, the atomic vibrations are so large that the atoms break completely free from the bonds that held them in groups. Once free, each atom flies through space on its own, changing direction only when it collides with another atom. This is what happens when a substance *vaporizes*.

Of course, the model you made has only one layer of atoms. Real samples of matter consist of many layers of atoms or molecules. Also, in your model the marbles do not move if you stop jiggling the tray. A better model would have the atoms moving all the time.

The kinetic theory can explain why some substances melt and vaporize at higher temperatures than others. It is because the forces or

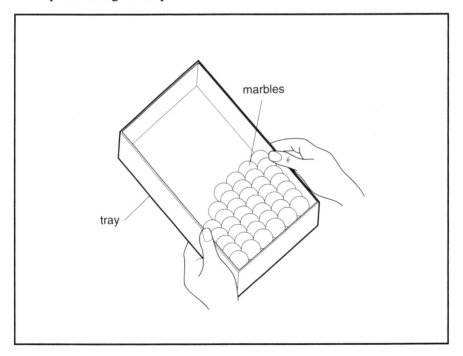

Figure 7-4) A model of matter.

chemical bonds between different types of atoms differ in strength. The stronger the bonds, the greater the degree of vibration needed to break them. Greater vibration means a higher temperature. The bonds between hydrogen molecules must be very weak because hydrogen vaporizes at -252°C (-422°F). On the other hand, the bonds between tungsten metal atoms must be very strong since it vaporizes at 5,927°C (10,700°F).

When a substance melts or boils, the heat added is used to break the bonds between atoms or molecules. This does not increase the speed of the atoms, and so there is no change in temperature when substances melt or boil.

The Triumph of the Kinetic Theory

You have found that the kinetic theory, which assumes that atoms are in constant motion, can explain temperature, melting, and vaporization. Can it also explain the rules of temperature change and the many temperature–related processes you investigated earlier? These include thermal expansion, the coldest temperature, conduction, heat capacity, and specific heat.

Before reading these explanations, review those rules and the processes mentioned above. Then, using the atomic model of matter and your imagination, try to explain them for yourself. Compare your explanations with the ones given below.

Thermal Expansion

According to the kinetic theory, the temperature of an object increases when the vibrations of its atoms get larger. But atoms with large vibrations take up more room than atoms with small vibrations. Therefore, objects expand as temperature rises. This is similar to the behavior of people at a party. A group engaged in conversation takes up only a small space. But if they start dancing, they quickly spread out and occupy more space.

The Coldest Temperature

As you have seen, temperature is a measure of the average speed of atoms and molecules. At -273°C (-459°F), according to the kinetic theory, atomic motion stops. Since a speed of zero is the smallest speed atoms can have, it also represents the smallest possible temperature. Therefore, -273°C is often referred to as absolute zero.

In fact, another temperature scale called the absolute scale assigns a value of zero to this temperature. On this scale temperatures are measured in *kelvins* (K) in honor of the Scottish scientist Lord Kelvin (William Thomson). Changes in temperature are the same as they are on the Celsius scale. However, there are no negative values on the absolute scale. On it, 0K equals -273.15°C, and 273.15K = 0°C.

Conduction

When the tip of a solid rod is placed in a flame, the atoms in the top vibrate faster. These faster moving atoms bump into neighboring atoms further along the rod. These atoms, in turn, bump into atoms still farther down the rod, and so on. As a result, the faster vibrations are soon transferred down the entire length of the rod. This is like a line of people holding hands. If the person at one end of the line pushes or pulls his or her neighbor, the push will be transferred along the entire line.

If thermal conduction results when atoms pass on their vibrations to neighboring atoms, then dense substances, such as metals, should have higher thermal conductivities than less dense substances. After all, the atoms of dense matter are close together. Gases, on the other hand, have low thermal conductivities because their atoms or molecules are far apart. They rely on collisions between distant atoms to transfer heat from one part of the gas to another. Since the atoms or molecules are far apart, the time required for this more rapid motion to spread through the gas is much greater than it is for solids and liquids, where the atoms or molecules are close together.

Of course, when we say that gas molecules are far apart, you must remember how small molecules are. Even though the molecules in a gas are ten times farther apart than they are in a liquid, there are still about 25,000,000,000,000,000,000 molecules in a cubic centimeter of air. This means the average distance between the molecules is only about 0.00000035 cm.

Heat Capacity and Specific Heat

As you have seen, the temperature of a substance is related to the average speed of its molecules. But we know that the amount of heat in an object, regardless of how we explain it, depends on the mass of the object. The more mass it has, the more heat it has at any given temperature. Warming 10 g of water by 1°C requires ten times as much heat as is needed to warm 1 g of water by 1°C. Consequently, the total heat in a sample of matter depends on its mass or the total number of atoms, which is where the mass is.

But how does a sample of matter acquire its heat unless it is transferred from a hotter object? You have seen that friction can produce heat. You may also know, through experience, that compressing a gas makes it warmer. When you pump air into a bicycle tire, the air becomes warmer. The reason is quite simple. When the piston in the pump pushes on the molecules or air, the molecules go faster. If molecules of matter move faster, it means their temperature has increased.

The same thing is true in the case of heat produced by friction. Friction involves the molecules in one surface pushing against the molecules in another surface. This pushing makes the molecules move faster, so their temperature increases.

Since heat capacity is the amount of heat required to raise the temperature of a sample of matter 1°C, the larger the sample of matter, the longer or harder we will have to push to attain the same temperature change.

Different substances require different amounts of heat to produce the same temperature change. In fact, we can use differences in specific heat to help us identify unknown substances. However, if we measure the amount of heat needed to raise the temperature of *equal numbers* of molecules by 1°C, the results are surprisingly similar for a variety of different substances. Less massive molecules move faster than heavier ones at the same temperature, but apparently some combination of mass and average speed is the same for all molecules.

The Rules of Temperature Change

In Chapter 3, you found the following rules of temperature change.

(1) When objects having different temperatures are put in contact, the cooler one gets warmer and the warmer one gets cooler until their temperatures become equal.

(2) The greater the difference in temperature between two touching objects, the faster their temperatures change.

(3) The greater the amount of something, the greater the temperature change it can cause in another object, and the less its own temperature changes in the process.

When two objects are touching, their vibrating atoms can knock against each other. In this way, the atoms of a hot object *conduct* their greater velocity to the atoms of the cooler object. The result is that the warm body cools and the cooler body warms. This transfer of atomic vibration continues until the atoms in both bodies reach the same degree of atomic vibration or the same temperature. This explains rule 1 of temperature change.

Rule 2 is explained by the fact that the greater the difference in atomic vibrations, the faster they are transferred to the cooler object. To understand why, imagine again a line of people with their hands joined. If the end person pulls or pushes gently, his or her neighbor will not move very fast. Therefore, the increased motion will be transferred along the line very slowly. However, if the end person pulls and pushes with a large force, the person pushed will acquire a greater speed and will, therefore, collide sooner with the next person. The same will hold for the next collision, and so on all the way down the line.

Rule 3 follows from the fact that a large object has many more vibrating atoms in it than a small one. Furthermore, a small decrease in the vibration of its many atoms can add up to a large increase in the vibration of the small object's atoms. This results in a large temperature increase in the small object without much effect on the large object. Many people blowing on a ball will change its speed a lot more than one person blowing on it.

A New Meaning for "Heat"

In this book you have learned that thermometers provide us with an objective way of measuring temperature. You then used thermometers to establish some rules of temperature change and to find out how heat differs from temperature.

You have also learned about Joseph Black's theory explaining the rules of temperature change. His fluid theory of heat successfully explained much about the behavior of heat. But as further investigations done by Black and by other scientists revealed new facts about heat, it became clear that the fluid theory had many flaws. It could not explain why denser substances are better conductors of heat than less dense ones. Nor could it account for the ability of radiant heat to travel through glass and air. And the question remained: How can a fluid be both weightless and invisible?

According to the kinetic theory, temperature is a measurement of the average speed of atoms or molecules, and heat is the *total* motion of all these particles. The kinetic theory of heat explains the behavior of heat without the need for an invisible, weightless fluid.

Evidence indicates that heat is not really a fluid, but this does not mean that the fluid theory must be discarded. Just as a story does not have to be true to teach a valuable lesson, a theory does not have to be perfect to be useful. Scientists and engineers routinely use the fluid theory of heat as a guide to designing scientific devices and industrial equipment. It is only when the fluid theory no longer serves to explain a particular process that it becomes necessary to use the kinetic theory.

A major flaw in the fluid theory of heat was the fact that no one could detect any evidence of a fluid that was weightless and invisible. The kinetic theory requires no imaginary fluid. It is based on the movement of atoms and molecules for which there is good evidence. In fact, special new microscopes, called scanning electron tunneling microscopes, enable us to see shadowlike images of atoms. Thus, the kinetic theory of heat is a better explanation of the way things really are.

The important thing for you to realize as you reach the end of this book is that science is forever changing. Theories are constantly being modified as investigations lead to new discoveries. And sometimes theories, like the fluid theory of heat, are supplemented by new theories that better explain some part of nature. As your study of science continues, you will find that the kinetic theory has flaws too, flaws that have led scientists to develop yet another theory to explain temperature and heat.

Bibliography

Beller, Joel. *So You Want to Do a Science Project*. New York: Arco, 1992.

Bombaugh, Ruth. *Science Fair Success*. Hillside, N.J.: Enslow, 1990.

Boyle, Desmond. *Energy*. New York: Silver Burdett, 1982.

Brown, Bob. *More Science for You: 112 Illustrated Experiments*. Blue Ridge Summit, PA: TAB, 1988.

Conway, Lorraine. *Energy*. Carthage, Ill.: Good Apple, 1985.

Gardner, Martin. *Entertaining Science Experiments with Everyday Objects*. New York: Dover, 1981.

Gardner, Robert. *Energy Projects for Young Scientists*. New York: Watts, 1987.

———. *Ideas for Science Projects*. New York: Watts, 1986.

———. *Save That Energy*. New York: Messner, 1981.

Gordon, Douglas. *Energy*. Pomfret, VT: David and Charles, 1984.

Maury, Jean Pierre. *Heat & Cold*. Hauppauge, NY: Barron, 1989.

Tocci, Salvatore. *How to Do a Science Fair Project*. New York: Watts, 1986.

Van Deman, Barry A., and McDonald, Ed. *Nuts and Bolts: A Matter of Fact Guide to Science Fair Projects*. Science Man Press, 1980.

Weaver, Elbert C. *Experiments: Properties of Gas and Heat Energy*. Arlington, VA: American Gas Association.

Webster, David. *How to Do a Science Project*. New York: Watts, 1974.

Wood, Robert W. *Physics for Kids: 49 Easy Experiments with Heat*. Blue Ridge Summit, PA: TAB, 1990.

Suppliers of Science Materials

The following companies supply the materials needed for the experiments in this book.

Carolina Biological Supply Co.
2700 York Road
Burlington, NC 27215

Central Scientific Co. (CENCO)
11222 Melrose Avenue
Franklin Park, IL 60131

Connecticut Valley Biological
Supply Co., Inc.
82 Valley Road
Southampton, MA 01073

Delta Education
P.O. Box M
Nashua, NH 03061

Edmund Scientific Co.
101 East Gloucester Pike
Barrington, NJ 08007

Fisher Scientific Co.
4901 W. LeMoyne Street
Chicago, IL 60651

Frey Scientific Co.
905 Hickory Lane
Mansfield, OH 44905

Gelatine Products
32 Morris Avenue
Glen Cove, NY 11542

McKilligan Supply Corp.
435 Main Street
Johnson City, NY 13790

Nasco Science
901 Janesville Road
Fort Atkinson, WI 53538

Nasco West Inc.
P.O. Box 3837
Modesto, CA 95352

Prentice Hall Allyn & Bacon
Equipment Division
10 Oriskany Drive
Tonawanda, NY 14150-6781

Schoolmasters Science
P.O. Box 1941
Ann Arbor, MI 48106

Science Kit & Boreal Laboratories
777 East Park Drive
Tonawanda, NY 14150-6782
or
P.O. Box 2726
Sante Fe Springs, CA 90670-4490

Wards Natural Science
Establishment, Inc.
5100 West Henrietta Road
P.O. Box 92912
Rochester, NY 14692

Index

About the Authors

Robert Gardner has written more than forty books for children of all ages, including earlier books in this series, *Science Projects About People* and *Science Projects About Light*. He has also written *Kitchen Chemistry, Science Around the House, Science in Your Backyard* (with David Webster), *Projects in Space Science, The Whale Watchers' Guide,* and *The Future and the Past* (with Dennis Shortelle). For many years, he was chairman of the science department at Salisbury School in Salisbury, Connecticut, where he taught physics, chemistry, biology, and physical science. For three years during the 1960s, he was a staff member of both the Elementary Science Study and the Physical Science Group at the Education Development Center in Newton, Massachusetts, where he worked on several National Science Foundation–funded projects involving the development of science materials. He now lives on Cape Cod with his wife, Natalie, where he enjoys writing, cycling, and whale watching.

Eric Kemer has been teaching physics, chemistry, and mathematics at St. Andrews School in Middletown, Delaware, since 1987. Prior to that, he was a materials research scientist for the Cabot Corporation in Boston, Massachusetts. When not teaching, coaching, writing, or, in his few spare moments, playing the harmonica, he and his wife Susan stay busy raising their three young children.